PERSPECTIVES ON ACADEMIC SUPPORT:
Adults with ADHD and Mental Health Challenges

PERSPECTIVES ON ACADEMIC SUPPORT:
Adults with ADHD and Mental Health Challenges

LAURA E. HUBBARD, PH.D.

PALMETTO
PUBLISHING
Charleston, SC
www.PalmettoPublishing.com

Copyright © 2025 by Laura E. Hubbard, Ph.D.

All rights reserved

No portion of this book may be reproduced, stored in a retrieval system, or transmitted in any form by any means–electronic, mechanical, photocopy, recording, or other–except for brief quotations in printed reviews, without prior permission of the author.

Paperback ISBN: 979-8-8229-7136-3
eBook ISBN: 979-8-8229-7137-0

DEDICATION

To my children, Elizabeth, Richard, and Jillian, with deepest love and gratitude.

TABLE OF CONTENTS

Introduction 1

Historical Perspective

Chapter 1| The Pendulum: A Brief History
of the Education and Care of
People with Psychiatric Disorders
in the United States. 7

Personal Perspective

Chapter 2| A Skype Story: Learning on
Two Sides of the World. 31

Adult College Student Perspectives

Chapter 3| Adult College Students with ADHD:
Giftedness, Creativity, and
Deep Engagement in Learning. 41
Chapter 4| Know Me: Lived Experiences of
Adult College Students with
ADHD and Coexisting
Psychiatric Disorders. 77

College Support Faculty Perspectives

Chapter 5| The Dance: Teacher/Learner
　　　　　　Lead and Follow 113
Chapter 6| Transformation:
　　　　　　Rewriting the Internal Script 157

References 165
Acknowledgements. 175
About the Author 177

INTRODUCTION

For three decades, I have had the profound honor to work with adult students with attention deficits (ADHD) and coexisting mental health challenges. As a college professor whose role it is to assist these students in reaching their academic goals, learning and teaching is transformational. Every day I have the opportunity to build relationships and to engage in the learning process with kind, courageous, and remarkable people. On the surface, the work is providing academic support for students who are attempting to finish undergraduate and graduate degrees and occasionally students who are trying to pass certificate programs in the trades. At first glance, the work seems straight forward. A student may need assistance in developing a sound writing process in order to complete academic papers or may need strategies to study for exams. These learned strategies may be products of student/teacher interactions, but the learning process itself is far more complex.

In my early work with this population, there was little in the research literature to guide my teaching practice. In response, I chose to do my own research and finished a

Ph.D. The research literature did expand over time, and I was grateful to read the work of scholars like Thomas Brown and Russell Barkley, which informed and continued to inform my understanding of my students. Above all, though, the students themselves were the most profound influences on developing a teaching practice responsive to student needs. This book is a collection of some of my recent research (each project vetted through the Institutional Review Board process), which I hope provides intimate access to the learning, teaching, and human experiences of adult students with ADHD and the professors who support them.

The first chapter is an overview of the history of psychiatric treatment in the United States. In working with my students over the years, it is consistently apparent that mental health difficulties that accompany attention deficits present daunting obstacles to achieving academic goals. In searching for best practices that support students who experience the day-to-day challenges of managing depression or anxiety, for example, I found that the history of psychiatric disorders treatment in the United States provides a context for contemporary adult student experiences.

Chapter two is an informal case study of my first time working virtually with a student. I am forever grateful to this student because the experience gave me the confidence to continue to learn and use technologies that support students who are unable to meet with me on campus. Technology offers a vehicle to work with students who are looking for support from any college or university. During the Covid-19 pandemic, students suddenly were required to complete all course work virtually. Technology now enables continuity of support for all my students.

The next two chapters are based on formal qualitative studies that my students initiated. In my teaching practice, I meet several times a week with each student individually. Then I meet once each week with students in groups. During these sessions, I frequently encounter students who demonstrate exceptional creative abilities. Through our group conversations, students often become aware of each other's creative strengths. One semester, a group of students wanted to examine this phenomenon further, and so the students and I decided to launch a qualitative study as one way to conduct that exploration.

The qualitative study in chapter four arose from students' frustrations that professors and various college personnel seemed not to understand or were unaware of the mental health difficulties they managed while complying with the demands of academics and the college environment. In order to edify the college community, the students decided to pursue a formal study in order to provide legitimacy to the information they wanted to share.

In chapter five, college professors, whose work specifically and intentionally supported adult students with ADHD, participated in a qualitative study. These professors, who were also my colleagues, brought a range of professional backgrounds to the adult learning and teaching experience. I relied on frequent collaborations with these colleagues to develop best practices that addressed adult learning needs. I felt it was important to formalize their contributions to the learning and teaching process of adult students with ADHD and coexisting psychiatric challenges by sharing their perspectives.

The final chapter discusses transformative learning as the model that study participants use in their teaching practice with adult students with complex ADHD. Transformative learning is foundational to the work and fosters an environment where the power structure between students and support faculty is shared; assumptions regarding learning and teaching are examined; and students and professors inhabit both learner and teacher roles as they work toward new personal and professional insights.

HISTORICAL PERSPECTIVE

CHAPTER 1

THE PENDULUM: A BRIEF HISTORY OF THE EDUCATION AND CARE OF PEOPLE WITH PSYCHIATRIC DISORDERS IN THE UNITED STATES

Introduction

From the Colonial Period to the present, the education and care of people with psychiatric disorders in the United States have swung back and forth several times like a pendulum. At times, families and communities support people with these disabilities and at other times people are left homeless or confined in institutions, including prisons. This brief history traces the Colonial Period to the beginning of the 21st century. The definitions of psychiatric disorders are addressed according to the historical period being discussed. The role of institutions, hospitals, residential facilities, private and public schools, and the deinstitutionalization movement are explored.

In her petitions to state legislatures from the 1840s to the 1870s, Dorothea Dix described the deplorable conditions under which people with psychiatric disorders lived. To the Massachusetts legislature she said:

> I come to present the strong claims of suffering humanity. I come as the advocate of helpless, forgotten, insane and idiotic men and women; of beings sunk to a condition from which the most unconcerned would start with real horror. (Dix, 1843, in Grob, 1994, p. 541)

To the New Jersey legislature, Dix stated in 1845 that she personally witnessed "in jails and poor-houses, and wandering at will over the country, large numbers of insane and idiotic persons" (Dix, 1845, in Grob, 1994, p. 541). In 1887, Dix told Tennessee lawmakers that the solution to the difficulties of the "insane" was to place them in "rightly organized hospitals" (p. 542). Throughout U.S. history, the care, treatment, and education of people with psychiatric disorders has shifted back and forth between some form of institutionalization and community-based efforts largely dependent on family involvement. When families have been unavailable and community-based support has had limited resources, people with psychiatric disorders have found themselves homeless. Treatment for people with psychiatric disorders has been determined throughout our history by the political, social, medical, educational, and economic frames of reference of the times.

This chapter surveys our U.S. society's response to the needs of people with psychiatric disorders. The terms or labels given to this population during the different time periods are used in the chapter to trace the evolution of the concept of mental disorder and help define those terms as currently used in the *Diagnostic and Statistical Manual of Mental Disorders, Fifth Edition (DSM-5).*

Labels and Definitions

The term *lunatic* was given to people with psychiatric disorders during the U.S. Colonial Period. At that time, the colonists thought that mental disorders were caused by exposure to a full moon either at birth or at some point in infancy (Lerner, 1996). This term was paired with *the insane* until the early 19th century when advocates of moral treatment began to consider this population as patients who were mentally ill.

Toward the end of the 19th century, a distinction was made between people with mental illness who were considered harmless and people with chronic mental illness who were considered violent and incurable. The former were released from what had evolved into large state mental hospitals, and people with chronic mental illness remained in custodial care (Lamb, 2001). By the turn of the twentieth century, the term *chronically mentally ill* began to include elderly people who demonstrated senility, poor people with mental illness, people with Huntington's chorea, people who were partially paralyzed, and people with brain tumors. In the early 1900s, all these people suffered from untreatable brain conditions. Many of these people with chronic mental illness died within five years of admittance to state hospitals; close to half died within the first year

(Grob, 1994). By the 1930s and 1940s, the population with chronic mental illness in large state mental hospitals was augmented by admissions of patients with chronic mental illness at younger and younger ages. These patients were identified as having schizophrenia and other forms of psychosis or illnesses that were characterized by loss of reality awareness and a disintegration of personality, thoughts, and feelings (Mechanic and Rochefort, 1990). The terms *mental illness*, *chronic mental illness*, *emotional disturbance*, and categories of mental illness such as psychosis and schizophrenia persisted through the twentieth century (Paige, 1998).

By the end of the twentieth century, the term *emotionally disturbed* and degrees of mental disorder such as *serious emotional disturbance* were used (IDEA, 1997). These were added to previous terms and categories. Various terms or labels were then formally articulated in federal and state laws, in diagnostic reference manuals, and in professional literature.

The following presents some of the formal definitions of mental disorder. In the science and medical communities, terms like *mental illness* and *mental disorder* indicate diagnosis and suggest treatment. Even within these two communities, there are no universally agreed-upon operational definitions (American Psychiatric Association, 2000). In the field of education, the term *emotional disturbance* is intended to be less stigmatizing (Wright, 2004) and suggests the need for educational services and accommodations.

According to the American Psychiatric Association in the *Diagnostic and Statistical Manual of Mental Disorders: DSM-5* (2013), the term *mental disorder* cannot be adequately defined because of the heterogeneous nature of the disorders included within that term. The *DSM-5* states, "Mental disorders do not always fit completely within the boundaries of a single disorder (p. xli)". However, the *DSM-5* offers the following guidelines for identifying behavioral or psychological patterns that deviate from normal functioning. A mental disorder is:

> A syndrome characterized by clinically significant disturbance in an individual's cognition, emotional regulation, or behavior that reflects a dysfunction in the psychological, biological, or developmental processes underlying mental functioning. Mental disorders are usually associated with significant distress or disability in social, occupational, or other important activities. (p. 20)

What follows this general definition in the *DSM-5* are detailed criteria for clinical diagnoses of a host of mental disorders.

The National Alliance for the Mentally Ill (NAMI), a citizen's advocacy group, defines mental illness as a term including "disorders of the brain that disrupt a person's thinking, feeling, moods, and ability to relate to others. Mental illnesses are brain disorders resulting in a diminished capacity for coping with the demands of life" (NAMI, 2004, p.1).

School systems continue to use the definition of emotional disturbance articulated in the federal law, *The Individuals with Disabilities Education Act* (IDEA, 1997) and IDEA 2004, as one reference to classify students needing special services. States like Massachusetts can have additional criteria to determine eligibility for special services. PL101-476 and PL108-446, *The Individuals with Disabilities Education Act,* define *emotional disturbance* as follows:

(i) The term means a condition exhibiting one of more or the following characteristics over a long period of time and to a marked degree that adversely affects a child's educational performance:

A. An inability to learn that cannot be explained by intellectual, sensory, or health factors.
B. An inability to build or maintain satisfactory interpersonal relationships with peers and teachers.
C. Inappropriate types of behaviors or feelings under normal circumstances.
D. A general pervasive mood of unhappiness or depression.
E. A tendency to develop physical symptoms or fears associated with personal or school problems.

(ii) The term includes schizophrenia. (Wright & Wright, 2000, p.140; IDEA, 2004, p.7).

The number of terms or labels for mental disorders indicates the complexities of the conditions within it and, subsequently, the complexities of providing education, care, and treatment for people living with mental disorders.

History of Care and Treatment from the Colonial Period through the 19th Century

Documents recording the care and treatment of *lunatics* during the Colonial Period are scarce (Lerner, 1996). The lack of records availability, as Lerner points out, may be due to the absence of scholarly investigation and interest. Documents that are available seem to indicate that our early colonists took care of their own within their communities.

The colonial population was sparse and widely distributed over rural settings. This rural feature of early America persisted through the Revolutionary War and the Civil War. During this period, *lunatics* or *distracted persons* were tolerated within families. Consequently, families primarily took care of the needs of their relatives with mental disorders. Those without families were boarded out to other families or supported the way paupers were supported, living in public almshouses (Grob, 1994). Based on the English Poor Laws written at the turn of the seventeenth century, most colonies enacted their own "Relief of the Poor" laws. The accepted principle of the time was that communities had an obligation to support people who were unable to survive without assistance. People with mental disorders were considered members of the poor (Hawes, 1991). Connecticut's poor laws enacted in 1699, for example, stated that relatives and estates of the insane were liable for their support (Brendel-Scriabine, 2005). As long as communities remained small, this system of caring for people with mental disorders was sustainable; however, the quality of care must have varied widely as it was highly dependent on the resources of the family.

Stewardship for people with mental disorders by families and local officials began to wane when populations in American communities began to increase and local resources for this population were depleted. Those who were seemingly harmless were permitted to roam about the country at will and those who were violent were put into prison. Again, Connecticut was typical of other states in its response to managing people with mental disorders at this time. In 1729, its legislature authorized local communities to confine the neglected insane (Brendel-Scriabine, 2005). The focus of care shifted from caring for people with mental illness to a focus on protecting the public. Unfortunately, sanctioned confinement was not supported with funding for facilities by the State of Connecticut. Consequently, families continued to try to manage their relatives, and more and more people with mental illness were put in prison or left homeless.

In the eighteenth century, the pendulum began to swing away from family and community-based care and support to confinement. Aside from individual families teaching and caring for their relatives, there was no structured plan for treating people with mental disorders in any public facility. Increasing populations created communities with more urban characteristics and strained limited state financial resources. Unfortunately, people with mental illness who had no families to care for them were left with no care. People of all ages with mental illness were crowded into almshouses and prisons, where their lives deteriorated (Luchins, 1990).

With overcrowding in prisons and almshouses and increased homelessness, the management of people with mental disorders became a social problem too large for local communities to handle at the turn of the nineteenth century. States were called upon to help communities manage people with mental illness. The nineteenth century was known for the use of insane asylums as the states' response to this social problem. By the Civil War, every state had at least one institution that housed this population (Grob, 1994). Dorothea Dix championed the establishment of insane or lunatic asylums across the country as humane places where people could receive special care. For forty years, she visited people with mental illness in prisons and in poor houses and then presented their cases before state legislatures across the country. Her testimonials regarding the deplorable conditions of the lives of confined and homeless people with mental illness influenced states to build public institutions for the purpose of managing this population. Patients of all ages were placed in these facilities (Luchins, 1990), which in the beginning housed no more than 250 patients at any given time.

In the early 1800s, a new approach was used to treat people with mental illness. Dr. Eli Todd was credited with introducing moral treatment when he founded the Hartford Retreat in 1821. Because of the apparent success of this treatment, superintendents, who were in charge of asylums, went to the Retreat for training (Luchins, 1988). Asylums were also influenced by utopian schemes, which proposed that given the correct environment, a person could be transformed to perfection and saved from the "sins" of fast-growing communities (Rothman, 1971). Given the "correct" environment in the asylum, the insane could be transformed into moral, productive citizens.

Moral treatment was the first systematic, organized approach in the country to attempt to rehabilitate the insane (Lamb, 2001). Moral treatment—which called for kindness at all times—was thought to advance moral discipline in the institution and to build the moral character of people with mental illness, who were now viewed as *patients* attended by physicians on a regular basis. The term *patient* identified a different, more human, status than that implied by the terms *insane* or *lunatic*. *Patients* were people who needed treatment, while the terms used in earlier times objectified people, stripping their humanness. As patients who were expected to return to the community, daily structured activities that included grooming and exercise, as well as educational and occupational activities, were prescribed for their moral reeducation (Lamb, 2001). A system of rewards and punishments was used as an incentive for patients to engage in their daily routines. Physicians kept close contact with the patients' families throughout the hospital stay. Because patients tended to improve in their overall functioning, it was thought that moral treatment produced cures. Indeed, asylum stays frequently lasted a matter of months, and patients were released based on the physicians' determination of changed social and moral behavior (Luchins, 1988). Dorothea Dix based her campaign for the humane care and treatment for people with mental illness on these small institutions that used moral treatment. She and other reformers of the day were successful at lobbying state legislatures to build more institutions at public expense (Lamb, 2001).

The period of moral treatment was short-lived. With the Industrial Revolution at the end of the nineteenth century, urban populations grew rapidly. Up until the Industrial Revolution, local communities and the states shared the expense of caring for and treating mentally ill patients. Overcrowding in the cities, which produced overwhelmingly poor living conditions in slums, made it impossible for individual communities to continue sharing the costs of asylums. Local money was needed to manage increased demands of a growing population (Grob, 1994). Consequently, states took over sole financial responsibility for people in asylums (Paige, 1998). States began to build large state hospitals, which housed up to 2000 patients, in order to accommodate the increasing numbers of admitted patients. Kirkbride, a Todd contemporary, who was responsible for the architectural design of many smaller asylums, adamantly opposed the building of the larger institutions, because they were intended to house chronically ill patients. It was Kirkbride's argument that housing large numbers of chronically ill patients could only lead to custodial care and eventually would lead back to the earlier patient abuses that were common before the introduction of moral treatment. States argued that establishing separate facilities for chronic patients was a better alternative than returning these patients to local almshouses, which was the available alternative of the day (Grob, 1994).

Several factors contributed to the increase in state hospital populations. State hospitals had no criteria for admittance (Grob, 1994). Since states shouldered all financial responsibility, cities sent any undesirable person who was identified as insane to the state hospital. Almshouses, which had always been used to house the poor, frequently housed the elderly poor. Prisons were overcrowded with criminals from poverty-stricken neighborhoods. Both almshouses and prisons were the financial responsibility of local communities. Since the poor, the elderly, and the criminals were identified as insane, local communities could admit all of these groups to state hospitals, which eased the financial burden on local communities (Paige, 1998). With the overwhelming problems of growing city populations, extreme poverty, and crowded state hospitals, the feasibility and enthusiasm for moral treatment gave way to pessimism that mental illness was incurable (Lamb, 2001). Kirkbride's concerns were realized when custodial care became the standard treatment approach to chronic patients in state hospitals.

Documentation is scarce on the treatment and care of insane children from the Colonial Period through the nineteenth century. The limited records that do exist indicate that children identified as insane were often homeless or living in almshouses. Children were also patients in asylums in the nineteenth century. They continued to reside in asylums and state hospitals after the Civil War and through the turn of the twentieth century. Public outcries at the living conditions of children residing in asylums and state hospitals resulted in the removal of some children to public orphanages, where living conditions were also poor. Children frequently died within the first five years of living in state hospitals and orphanages (Lerner, 1996).

By the end of the nineteenth century and through the turn of twentieth century, the pendulum had completed its first full swing. Patients with mental illness included chronically mentally ill patients, especially poor chronically mentally ill patients, criminals, and poor elderly. This conglomeration of people was housed in the most restricted and segregated setting of large institutions and given minimal care and treatment. The living conditions in the large institutions were similar to those against which Dorothea Dix and other reformers of her time had protested almost a century earlier. It should be noted that those families who had the resources to care for their relatives with mental illness continued to do so throughout the nineteenth century.

Care and Treatment in the Twentieth Century

During the period extending approximately from one decade before to one decade after the turn of the twentieth century, several factors converged to put pressure on state hospitals to account for their treatment of patients with chronic mental illness. During the Industrial Revolution, physicians began treating patients using empirical research derived from the scientific method. There was pressure on state hospitals by the medical community to allow access to state hospital patients for the purpose of gathering empirical information on the functioning of the brain. The medical community criticized physicians who worked in state hospitals for using outdated methods of patient care that were not empirically based. The practice of psychiatry was no longer restricted to state hospitals; physicians treated patients with less severe mental illness in their offices within their communities (Luchins, 1988).

Social work was becoming an accepted discipline. Social workers of the time, like nineteenth-century advocates of moral treatment, identified problems in the community as causing mental illness. When certain environmental problems were solved, many mental illnesses could be prevented. Social workers put pressure on state hospitals to gain access to the hospitals and their patients in order to test their theories using state hospital environments. The field of psychology was also emerging. Psychologists such as Alfred Binet were developing methods to test intellectual functioning. The psychologists also applied pressure to state hospitals to gain access to the hospitals' patients to test their theories. Unfortunately, none of these disciplines focused on improving treatment for state hospital patients (Mechanic and Rochefort, 1990).

Living conditions at state hospitals came under scrutiny at the turn of the century. In 1908, Clifford Beers, a businessman and Yale graduate, published *A Mind That Found Itself*, an autobiographical account of his treatment in Connecticut state hospitals. After his release, Beers wanted to reform the entire state hospital system in the United States. He founded the Connecticut Society for Mental Hygiene, which within a year became the National Committee for Mental Hygiene to educate Americans about the issues of mental illness and promote a shift in perspective from the idea of illness to health. In 1920, the Committee presented Congress with a model of commitment laws. The Committee eventually merged with the later established National Mental Health Foundation and the Psychiatric Foundation in 1950 to form the National Association of Mental Health (NAMH) which was the early relative of the present day National Mental Health Association (NMHA) (NMHA 2005).

In the 1930s, during the Great Depression, concerned mental health professionals and self-advocacy groups such as the National Committee for Mental Hygiene wrote about neglectful and abusive practices in state hospitals. Because of the Depression, previously insufficient funding to support state hospitals and living conditions only worsened (NMHA, 2005).

By World War II, mental hospitals significantly lost credibility with the public as a place to treat patients with mental illness. According to Goessling (2000), several factors contributed to this. The horrors of Nazi Germany made institutionalizing people unacceptable. World War II veterans suffering from mental illness seemed to make progress when treated in community centers and on an outpatient basis. The development and use of psychotropic medications enabled patients to control their symptoms outside hospital settings. Also, the establishment of a federal welfare system provided financial support for individual patients to live within the community. Psychiatrists left institutional environments to work in community-based care facilities and private practice. Prior to the 1940s, this kind of care was primarily available to children of families who were able to afford this treatment (Mechanic and Rochefort, 1990). The pendulum was poised to swing away from institutional care toward community-based care and the beginnings of the deinstitutionalization movement.

By the 1950s, states began enacting laws that strengthened funding for community-based treatment facilities, even though little research existed at the time to demonstrate the efficacy of this treatment. California passed the Short-Doyle Act and New York passed the Community Mental Health Services Act, both of which provided state funding for outpatient clinics. According to Grob (1994), psychiatrists were the strongest advocates of community-based mental health centers. They promoted the view that early intervention through local clinics prevented hospitalizations. By 1959, there were 1400 mental health clinics nationwide providing services for 502,000 patients, of whom 208,000 were under age eighteen.

In the 1950s and 1960s, the civil rights movement had begun in the United States. Chief Justice Warren ruled in the *Brown v. Board of Education* (1954) Supreme Court decision that segregating children in public schools based on race violated the Equal Protection Clause of the Fourteenth Amendment to the Constitution, even where the physical facility, curriculum, and quality of teachers were said to be equal (Goessling, 2000). This ruling opened the door to examine segregation practices throughout American society (Stainback and Stainback, 1996). The District

Court decision in *Mills v. Board of Education of District of Columbia* (1972) established that children with disabilities were entitled to an appropriate education regardless of the severity of their disability and were also entitled to compensatory services (Wright and Wright, 2000). This was the first court decision in the nation to mandate that all children with disabilities had a constitutional right to public education, though institutionalized children were excluded from a public education.

The civil rights movement of the 1960s and the Supreme and district court decisions helped to develop policy that was intended to improve the human condition of institutionalized people with mental illness. According to Mechanic and Rochefort (1990), President John F. Kennedy proposed to Congress in 1963 a national community mental health program. Congress consequently enacted the Community Mental Health Centers (CMHC) Act of 1963. The goal of CMHC was to relocate segregated, custodial care patients to community-based centers. The deinstitutionalization movement and community mental health movement had officially begun. The National Institute of Mental Health (NIMH) produced research studies regarding the adverse effects of institutionalizing people with mental illness. Although the accuracy of these studies was unclear, lawyers now versed in the civil rights laws of the 1960s took up the cause of the civil rights of institutionalized patients. The challenge to civil commitment, or institutionalizing patients without their consent, became the foundation of patients' rights to the least restrictive alternative to state hospitals.

Grob (1994) identified several assumptions that supported the idea that it was possible to treat all mental illnesses in community mental health clinics and centers. First, it was assumed that psychiatrists who were working in the community and in private offices were competent in addressing the needs of patients who were severely and chronically mentally ill. In fact, unlike their state hospital counterparts who were criticized for outdated treatment approaches, these psychiatrists had little to no experience at all in working with such patients. Second, it was assumed that formerly hospitalized patients had homes and families with whom to live. It was also assumed that families had the skills to care for their mentally ill family members and were able to take responsibility for them. Another assumption was that having a family member with mental illness living at home would not create undue financial and emotional hardships for the family. The reality was that by 1960, three-quarters of the patient population, who in previous years would have resided in mental hospitals, had no homes at all. Mechanic and Rochefort (1990) further stated that there was a false assumption that there were adequate numbers of community-based centers to meet the needs of the growing numbers of patients present in the community.

From the mid-nineteenth century until the 1960s, mental health care and policy had been left to individual states. With CMHC, the federal government shared financial support with states and made policy for the care and treatment of patients with mental illness. Beginning with the mid-1960s through the 1970s, deinstitutionalization expanded rapidly as a result of Medicaid, an expanded welfare system, low-income housing, Social Security disability insurance, and food stamps. Federal financial assistance made it possible to support patients within the community. The CMHC concept of community-based facilities provided for inpatient care, outpatient care, emergency care, partial hospitalization, and community education about mental illness (Paige, 1998).

By the beginning of the 1980s, during the first Reagan administration, funding and policy-making was given back to the states as the Alcohol, Drug Abuse, and Mental Health block grant. Only half of the proposed community centers had been established nationwide. Funding for all the previous federal subsidies was severely cut back. Homelessness increased among this population (Mechanic and Rochefort, 1990).

In response to diminished federal support, fewer state hospital placements, and limited CMCH's, small private hospitals and general care hospitals provided treatment for patients with mental illness in new special psychiatric units (Mechanic and Rochefort, 1990). Supervised group homes, nursing homes for both young and elderly people with mental illness, supervised apartments, and residential care facilities for children provided living arrangements for chronically mentally ill patients. Hospitals provided acute care. All of these facilities competed for resources. Homelessness among youth with mental illness continued to grow, and drug abuse among this population compounded this problem. The pendulum was about to swing back. Communities were having difficulty taking care of their mentally ill populations. As in the days of Dorothea Dix, many mentally ill people, including children, were wandering homeless.

The Twenty-first Century

The National Alliance for the Mentally Ill (NAMI), one of the few advocacy organizations for people with mental disorders, published several accounts of a Congressional investigative report presented July 7, 2004. According to the report, thousands of youths with mental illness were put in juvenile detention centers to await mental health services. Mental health advocates, prison officials, and juvenile court judges offered three solutions: more community mental health centers partly funded by Medicaid; more cooperation between police officials and mental health service providers; and more extensive insurance coverage (Pear, 2004; Werner, 2004).

Even forty years after the CMHC Act of 1963, there continues to be a demand for adequate numbers of community-based mental health facilities and adequate funding to support these facilities. Deinstitutionalization is not yet accomplished, because a shortage of mental health treatment alternatives to institutionalization persists. As in the time just prior to the establishment of the asylum, children and adults with mental illness are still put in prisons. DeHart and Iachini (2019) report, "The number of mentally ill incarcerated persons is continuing to climb, and the severity of their illnesses is also increasing" (p. 457), which supports The Treatment Advocacy Center's (2016) research findings. Grohs (2017) adds that not only are the numbers rising but, "By now it's common knowledge that correctional facilities have become the housing unit for millions of people with mental health issues (p. 17)". The pendulum swings back to institutionalization.

Summary

This chapter presented a short history of the care and treatment of people with mental disorders in the United States from the Colonial Period to the present. Documentation for this study was limited; researchers such as Grob, Mechanic, and Lamb complained about gaps in documentation in their studies. In tracing the history, from colonial times through deinstitutionalization, a cycle of care and treatment seemed to emerge. When financial and physical resources were strained while trying to meet the needs of people with mental disorders in the community, homelessness among this population, including the young, increased. Next there appeared to be a trend toward confining homeless people, including young people, in prisons. In the past, warehousing of large numbers of people with mental disorders in institutions and prisons was the solution to the problem of caring for those with mental illness.

In telling this history, the labels of the times were identified as each period was discussed. At the end of the twentieth century, there were no universally agreed-upon terms among educators, mental health advocates, and mental health providers. NAMI used the term *mental illness*, educators used the term *emotionally disturbed*, and mental health providers used *mental disorders*. A danger of labeling was the possibility of stigmatizing individuals. Another aspect of the terminology problem was identifying a label descriptive enough to indicate a path for care and treatment. This seemed impossible given the heterogeneous nature of characteristics among this population. One person with schizophrenia, for example, might transition to the community with support and manage his life; another person with schizophrenia with similar support may continue to struggle to manage her life in a community (Grob, 1994).

In the twenty-first century, the pendulum will probably continue to swing as mental health professionals, physicians, educators, and lawmakers grapple with the complex issues of the care, treatment, and education of people with mental disorders. The political, social, medical, educational, and financial contexts for providing services for people with mental illness will likely continue to influence the quality and availability of appropriate services for this population.

PERSONAL PERSPECTIVE

CHAPTER 2

A SKYPE STORY: LEARNING ON TWO SIDES OF THE WORLD

Introduction

Despite my skepticism about the use of Skype, Facetime, or Zoom as delivery systems for learning and teaching, a student and I took a risk to engage in the learning process from opposite sides of the world. The student, who had attention deficits and learning disabilities, risked trusting a professor to help him learn to learn, and I risked trusting a different delivery system to help the student. The surprising result was that by using Skype, the student and I were able to build a strong relationship, fundamental to the learning/teaching process, and we both connected to new learning.

The Story

My first introduction to Jay, a young adult student, was through his mother. She had simply telephoned me looking for information regarding the academic support program for adult college students that I coordinated for a small liberal arts college near Boston, Massachusetts. Jay's mother had researched, but was unable to find such a program in her country that specifically supported adult college students with attention deficits (ADHD) and learning disabilities. She finally learned of the existence of my program from a friend of hers, whose young adult son had also been a part of the program. During our half-hour conversation, I described the support services available to adult students, and she disclosed some of Jay's challenges. After ending the conversation, I really did not expect to hear from Jay's mother again since she and her family lived outside the United States, on the other side of the globe.

A few months passed and Jay's mother contacted me again stating that she was visiting the Boston area and would like to make an appointment to meet in person. We talked in my office for over an hour about her concerns. Jay lived at home with his parents, was extremely gifted intellectually, and stuck. He had been working the same part-time job for four years: a job that held no future for him. Although unhappy in his place of employment, Jay remained in the job because of its familiarity and predictability. Indeed, he had friends and a girlfriend; however, Jay spent many hours in front of the computer or sleeping.

Jay had had a comprehensive neurodevelopmental assessment completed when he was eighteen. While the testing did not explicitly state that Jay had ADHD, the testing summary identified characteristics shared by people with diagnosed ADHD. This was of increasing concern to Jay's mother, as well as her concerns regarding his diminishing self-esteem. She felt that the small college where I worked would be a good fit for Jay because he would get the help he needed from the support program. Unfortunately, Jay's mother was certain that he would be unwilling to attend a college so far from home. At this point, her son was unwilling to take college classes, which was worrisome since his cognitive testing placed him in the very superior range.

Several tasks confronted this mother. One was to discuss with her son the opportunity to address his learning challenges and encourage him to try an academic activity that could stimulate his fine thinking with the hope of moving him toward a more satisfying direction for his life. Then there was the logistical challenge of accessing the Boston area, with its small liberal arts college with the academic support program.

I waited for Jay or his mother to contact me once his mother returned home. Based on our meeting, I assumed that Jay would be encouraged to attend the college where I worked in order to enroll in the adult support program while working toward his degree. Through an email, Jay stated he was still not ready to make such as large move both geographically and emotionally; however, the notion to begin exploring his learning difficulties was of interest. The means to make this happen across continents, I thought, was going to be very difficult. For more than 25 years, my practice had always involved one-to-one, face-to-face work with adults who have learning disabilities and/or ADHD and had taken place in my office. At Jay's mother's suggestion, I was now going to try to work with her son over Skype.

I set up my first Skype account, and Jay and I agreed via email on an appointed meeting time. For the next year and a half, we met every week at 8:30, which was 8:30 a.m. Jay's time and 8:30 p.m. my time. Admittedly, I was nervous anticipating our first meeting. I worried about sustaining the technical connection. I worried about my ability to build a relationship, which is the core of my work with students, while using a foreign medium such as Skype. I thought I would be unable to read the nonverbal communication I was accustomed to assessing in my office with students who were physically present. I worried most of all that Jay would be ill at ease with me under the distance conditions.

As it turned out, Skype was a very reliable means of connecting with my student, and it did, indeed, support the one-to-one and face-to-face work that facilitated progress. During our

first meeting, we identified some of Jay's strengths and decided on some initial goals. Between the first and second meeting, Jay emailed me his cognitive testing. The second meeting involved discussing his learning profile according to his testing. We began an ongoing conversation about adult attention deficits, and I emailed Jay research literature about ADHD. We explored the ways in which he experienced his own ADHD and discussed the research.

Slowly, after much resistance, Jay became more willing to write short pieces, which were responses to writing prompts. The writing presented a previously undiagnosed language-based learning disability. There were errors characteristic of dyslexia, which included omissions, substitutions, and sequencing difficulties. Expository writing was one of the greatest sources of challenge that Jay encountered throughout his academic life. He had difficulty initiating the writing and sustaining effort on his writing. Once started, Jay had difficulty articulating his many rich ideas coherently. As a result, writing was an effort that involved tremendous anxiety and was a persistent threat to his view of himself as a competent learner. Skype provided an opportunity to work back and forth on Jay's writing in real time.

With some understanding of his learning strengths and challenges, Jay and I discussed registering for an online college course of his choice in order to practice and expand his learning competencies. In our initial meeting, Jay had asserted that his academic strengths lay in science and math. We decided that we would both enroll in a noncredit online course about neurons and the brain. This class was carefully selected in order to provide Jay with subject matter that was intellectually stimulating and challenging. Neuroscience was of particular interest to him and the course involved calculus, as well. The class consisted of weekly lectures, homework assignments, textbook reading assignments, quizzes, and a final. Throughout the online course, Jay and I collaboratively identified and evaluated best study practices for him to utilize including note taking, test preparation, test taking, reading comprehension, and time management. We finished and passed the course.

Jay and I also explored, in depth, both the positive and negative effects of ADHD on his daily life and on his learning. Because Jay struggled with sustained effort and he frequently felt anxious and overwhelmed, Jay was evaluated for medication and he engaged a therapist. With the addition of medication and counseling to his new learning competencies, Jay decided to apply to university. Our next chapter over Skype focused on exploring possible university matches. Together we examined several college websites. I supported Jay's efforts to develop questions to ask at a college interview, to set appointments with college admissions counselors, and to arrange college tours. I helped Jay to hold himself accountable for completing his college applications on time. Since written expression tapped into Jay's learning disability, writing the college essay was a source of anxiety, which was exacerbated by the notion that the essay was an important component of the college application. Skype sessions were dedicated to reviewing Jay's writing process, reinforcing his new skills, and working through his struggles to initiate the writing. After visiting Jay's college choices, Jay applied to and was accepted by a university that offered part-time classes to adult-aged students. This university also provided tutoring for students with documented learning disabilities. Jay completed a math class and received an "A" for his first university grade.

Several years have now passed since I worked with Jay. Facetime and Skype have become routine mediums in my work with adult students with LD/ADHD. I continue to work with students who reside in other parts of the United States, as well as other parts of the world.

Summary

Admittedly, this project was launched despite my own skepticism, which was based upon my assertion that working with complex adult learners had to take place in person. I worried if Skype would be enough to address the many learning needs of my student who lived on the other side of the globe. It had been my experience that building a trusting relationship with students was fundamental to the students' ability to make progress. I could offer all the learning strategies I knew to be helpful, but if students did not trust me, they would never trust that the strategies would help them and therefore never try them. In my practice, it is important that students feel authentically seen and deeply understood. I hoped that Skype would not limit this.

Jay was right at home with Skype and online technology in general, which greatly reduced my concern about possible restrictiveness in working together. Our weekly meetings produced the forward movement that Jay had desired and, indeed, was ready to undertake. He learned about his strengths and challenges, connected with a therapist, continued with medication, applied to and was accepted by a college of his choice, and developed competencies that built on his strengths and better positioned him for college success. For my part, I learned to use Skype and other technologies effectively. The work with Jay was very satisfying, in part, because I took a risk that led to satisfying outcomes. Through Jay's instruction, I utilized the features of Skype that included working on writing pieces and sharing research in real time. I took a challenging online course, and although a strategy for checking comprehension was to have Jay describe the concepts he understood, I was grateful for his comprehension because it augmented mine. Most importantly, though, it was clear that building a teaching-learning relationship was possible using Skype. Jay would have been unwilling to attempt anything that I suggested, and he would not have shared his ideas regarding his ambitions, obstacles to those ambitions, and remedies if we did not develop such a relationship.

From time to time, I receive updates from Jay. He has moved out of his parents' house, has a new job, and has married his girlfriend. Jay also persists with his studies. Maybe someday we can meet in person.

ADULT COLLEGE STUDENT PERSPECTIVES

CHAPTER 3

ADULT COLLEGE STUDENTS WITH ADHD: GIFTEDNESS, CREATIVITY, AND DEEP ENGAGEMENT IN LEARNING

Roger's Perspective

"THE FUNNIEST THING about doing anything creative in my case writing is that it almost feels like I don't do it. What I mean by that is when I sit down to write, my eyes are staring at the computer screen, my hands are on the keyboard, but my brain is elsewhere. I've stepped out for a while. When I come back, there's words on the screen; there's words on the virtual page. It's basically allowing myself to go into that trancelike state: whatever gets splattered on the page happens. It's a cool feeling, though. It is. I almost feel rested when I come out of it.

It's a very strange experience to let a piece sit for a couple of days and then go back and read it as an observer, as a reader, not as an author. I think, 'Wait a second, I wrote that? It's actually not bad! I don't even remember writing that!' Because I'm not there when I'm writing. I'm just in whatever space I'm in. It's a very strange phenomenon."

Introduction

The process of learning and teaching necessitates creative practices both small and large in order to help adult students with attention deficits (ADHD) find sustainability and satisfaction in their academic work. In part, this is achieved by discovering and supporting emerging competencies, which in turn enables students to reimagine their internal scripts. They can recalibrate their internal narratives to include competent learners and achievers.

Throughout my teaching practice working with adult college students with ADHD and co-existing psychiatric disorders, I frequently encounter students who are gifted cognitively and highly creative. Inconsistent academic performance, difficulties progressing toward degree completion, and histories of irregular attendance in previous colleges are also common experiences among these students. The incongruity of strong potential and limited demonstrated achievement underlies significant levels of distress.

Several students in my teaching practice wanted to examine in a very deliberate way this paradox of high intellectual and creative potential and limited academic achievement. To explore this phenomenon, the students and I launched a qualitative research project. In the context of creativity, they wanted to understand their learning strengths and challenges, examine their learning processes, and identify learning and teaching practices that might better support their desire to engage the curriculum in meaningful ways. Qualitative interviews provided the space for these students' voices.

The students and I began our study by examining some of the research literature on creativity. According to Gnezda (2015):

> Creativity is a cognitive, emotional, manipulative experience that is accessible to all people. Creativity is cognitive because it is about innovating and developing ideas and occurs via specialized mental processes. Emotional because emotions are integral in the creative process. Manipulative because ideas present themselves, tempting the creator to quit working on the first idea in order to jump into new, more seductive ones. (p. 47)

Robinson (2015) states, "Creativity is the process of having original ideas that have value" (p. 118). Creativity begins with the imagination, which is the process of "bringing to mind" new ideas that are not externally experienced and concludes with the expression of the new idea. Gnezda (2015) and Robinson assert that creativity requires the hard work of critical thinking in order to evaluate, refine, make new connections, and persist with the work. Robinson and Gnezda agree that motivating forces for creativity are curiosity and discovery where creativity can be a pathway to new learning. In order to realize the products of the imagination, people acquire new skills.

When initiating a task, highly creative people usually start at low levels of energy and remain at low levels while engaging in lengthy processes to select ideas. During this low energy stage, time is spent on inward thinking where the person appears outwardly to be unproductive. At the second phase, the brain's arousal elevates to execute the idea. Ideas merge, which can be experienced as inspiration (but time may be too short to finish the process.) The final phase of the creative process is implementation or communicating the idea. This may consist of intense production as well as frustrating moments when obstacles or problems are encountered, requiring persistence in order to finish (Gnezda, 2015). The production of college academic assignments can be difficult for adult college students with ADHD who are highly creative partly due to fluctuations in energy levels.

Because creative thinkers engage in deep states of thought, sometimes trance-like concentration, they lose track of time. Gnezda (2015) refers to "deep engagement" in the creative process as experiencing a "trance-like state." They appear to be procrastinators because their brains favor a long idea process, and the energy necessary to implement the idea kicks in late. They seem disorganized and forgetful because, in order for their minds to carry around great thoughts and their next creations, they may spend less of their mental resources on tasks such as organizing their desks or checking their calendars for appointments. The outwardly observable behaviors of creative thinkers are also seemingly the behaviors of people with ADHD. Adult students with ADHD show difficulty initiating tasks, miss academic deadlines, can experience the passage of time in nonlinear ways, can appear to be outwardly unproductive when first engaging in academic activities and then demonstrate last-minute bursts of energy to complete assignments.

Amabile (2013) identifies four components that come together to enable an individual's creativity, three internal components and one external component. The internal components are: a person's existing skills and knowledge that support new learning needed for creative tasks; an individual's capacity for risk taking; and a sense of curiosity to try new tasks that comprise the internal elements of creativity. The external component is the person's environment. The level of creativity reflects the level of functioning of all components. Low levels of functioning support everyday occurrences of creativity such as identifying solutions to problems. High levels of functioning enable high levels of creativity such as the creation of art, inventions, and science discoveries. Amabile also includes passion: passion for the work and attachment to the work because the work is hard. "People are most creative when they feel motivated primarily by the interest, enjoyment, satisfaction, and challenge of the work itself" (Amabile, 2013, p. 4). The study participants are often challenged when addressing the demands of their daily lives (Brown, 2015). In addition to high functioning moments when they create visual art or poetry, they engage Amabile's (2013) low level of creative functioning to solve the problems they encounter when interacting with family members, friends, and work and school environments.

Brown (2012) states, "When failure is not an option, we can forget about learning, creativity, and innovation" (p. 15). Adult college students with ADHD and creative gifts experience frequent failure in school and often attend multiple colleges. Rather than attributing failure as an opportunity for new learning, the participants in this study state that they feel "stupid" when experiencing the discrepancy between their own potential and progress toward degree completion. They have difficulty navigating the "one size fits all…linear" (Robinson, 2015, p. 209) education. Generating ideas is rarely a problem; they have complications with production exacerbated by the challenges of meeting linear requirements such as deadlines. Consequently, these students connect "their self-worth to what they produce" (Brown, 2012, p. 65). Self-worth is further confounded by a "conflict between their picture of themselves as exceptionally bright and talented and their view of themselves as disappointing failures" (Brown, 2014, p. 39). Despite this conflict, the students in this study have the courage to persist with their education. Their courage is further demonstrated by initiating this study and by their openness to sharing their intimate thoughts and feelings. Brown (2012) calls this the strength of vulnerability.

The Study

Five men and three women, ages 22 to 27, volunteered for this study. Roger, Robert, and Mike were writers; Jason, Helen, and Lisa were visual artists; Jane was a musician; and Ben was a mathematician. Each person's high cognitive ability as measured by the Wechsler Adult Intelligence Scale 4th Edition (WAIS-IV), was equal to or greater than 120 on the Verbal Comprehension Index and/or the Perceptual Reasoning Index. All the participants had a documented diagnosis of attention deficit disorder, which presented a host of challenges that competed with their potential to be highly successful. At minimum, this competition challenged their endurance to work toward a college degree, and maximally obstructed their desires to engage in satisfying intellectual and creative work. The eight adult college student participants took part in the study to explore their strengths and the contributions these strengths made to engagement in learning; the external and internal foils to their learning; and factors that facilitated and supported fulfilling learning experiences.

The ninety-minute qualitative interviews with the participants revealed an overarching theme of connection. Fifteen codes clustered under three main categories, which were dynamic and interrelated. They emerged from the data in the interview transcriptions: connection to self, connection to others, and connection to academic work. Connection was particularly important to this group of students in order to experience satisfying academic engagement. The participants' understanding of themselves facilitated connection to professors, which enabled more, and deeper, connections to the work and to their learning.

Connection to Self

Self-awareness

The eight participants presented in-depth reflections regarding their inner lives. The participants described their battles with executive function disorders in generating assignments and detailed challenges in their learning processes. For example, Ben stated, "I know I'm more capable doing certain things than a lot of people. If I find the right field, I can be extremely successful. But, in the majority of things, I struggle more than people realize." Ben referred to his mathematical gifts, but demonstrated problems in many other areas in his academic life. Robert revealed his difficulty with sustained attention, "It's part of my everyday life. I realize that my attention is waning or that I'm starting to go into my own little la-la land. I am conscious of my unconsciousness. I am conscious of me slipping." Robert was committed to working on his awareness of his attention challenges. "By the time I'm done with college, I'd like to have grasp of myself; of what buttons I can push to get me to go in a certain direction; how to control myself. That's the end goal."

Intelligence

These students experienced frustration with their understanding of their gifts and the inability to witness evidence of these gifts. The participants stated that they were "smart" and that they relied on their cognitive abilities to rescue them or enable them to avoid school work until the last possible moment, assuring themselves that their abilities would produce high quality work quickly. Jane realized that the labor involved in production of assignments such as typing on a keyboard, could only be as fast as she could type, saying:

> I rely on my ability to be smart a little too much, because I want my intelligence alone to defy the laws of space and time. On one hand, maybe I can think up the whole paper in 10 minutes, but can I execute it in 10 minutes? No.

Often the participants did not acknowledge their cognitive gifts because the evidence of producing school work in a timely manner or remembering to complete and submit assignments presented contradictory evidence to their notion of high intelligence. Ben tried to untangle the mystery of completing school work that he had observed in other students. He stated:

> There's a common acceptance of what a successful academic achievement is, but I haven't experienced typical academic achievement. Mine is a different process, differently executed. I think there is a format that's common knowledge, but I can't pair it up with how I do it. I'm pretty hard on myself too.

Several participants identified difficulties with linear sequential thinking that thwarted attempts to produce school work, thus resulting in serious consequences. "It's hard to meet deadlines," complained Mike. "It's hard to complete steps, every step of the process on time. And that leads to long-lasting problems with professors, the universities, departments, whatever."

When some participants were acknowledged for an academic accomplishment, only then did their belief system begin to change. Jason declared:

> My third semester here, I made Dean's List! I didn't even know I was going to, but that was pretty awesome. That showed I was capable of doing it. Everyone kept saying 'your IQ's stupid good!' I felt exactly that, stupid, because I was never successful in school, ever.

When Mike was able to engage in an assignment that was meaningful to him, he found success, saying:

> I gave a really good presentation on something that had affected me. I put my heart into it; I put real work into it. It got me rewarded. It got me a big compliment, and it got me a good grade. Having the reinforcement that what you were doing was better than you thought, turns your thinking to, 'Oh, maybe I'm not such a bad student.'

Memory

Participants described their difficulties with memory and the impact their memory challenges had on school work and learning experiences. Difficulties with working memory is a hallmark of ADHD. Lisa moaned, "My memory is awful. It definitely keeps me from productive learning. A lot of times it will go in one ear and directly out the other because there's too much information in my head." Jason expressed a constant underlying anxiety that accompanied memory problems, which contributed to his overall stress. He reported:

> It's the endless loop of thinking about it (an assignment) and forgetting about it over and over and over again. It pops in my head, I worry, and then I forget. It pops in my head later down the road when it's crunch time. Then it's nose to the grindstone and pray that I can get something done; half the time I don't…When I've gotten in the thick of things, you start to see I forget little things here and there that get me in a bind, and I have to crawl my way out.

Several participants described issues with trying to establish new habits of mind in order to augment their difficulties with memory, particularly short-term memory. Ben and Helen frequently forgot to write down their assignments. Ben noted that by not establishing this habit, he remembered to do the work too late, and his assignments "piled up and spiraled out." Helen was more consistent in utilizing an assignment journal; however, if she was interrupted when recording an assignment, she admitted, "I'll completely forget about it." Jason relied on post-it notes,

"Even if I have a book, which I do, I don't use it all the time because I'll forget where it is."

Mental Health

During the course of their interviews, the participants mentioned that they grappled with mental health difficulties, which were multiple and complex. They disclosed problems with depression, anxiety, obsessive compulsive disorder, Tourette's Syndrome, and bipolar disorder. These were issues they continued to manage while confronting the requirements of being students. Historically, their mental health had presented serious obstacles to working toward their college degrees. Jane disclosed:

> What gets in the way of doing the things I'm supposed to do is either I feel like it doesn't matter if I go to class or not; it doesn't matter if I turn in my work or not. I'll get depressed about things and get discouraged and then I won't want to leave my room.

When he was overwhelmed with anxiety, Robert stopped going to class, stating:

> That was my downfall in almost every academic setting where I didn't succeed. I would get in over my head in terms of getting behind, and then I wouldn't want to show up to class. I would completely disconnect myself, and I would block it out of my brain. I would know as I was walking away from class that it was the wrong

thing to do, that I shouldn't be doing it, but I would do it anyway.

Roger revealed the way ruminating presented a barrier to generating school work:

> Interpersonal things usually feed my depression, which then feeds the ADD, which feeds ambivalence. I internalize a lot of things that go on around me and will mull over them. The internal arguing happens, which makes a big period of time where nothing will happen.

Jason suffered from, "A lot of anxiety throughout my life. I'm always anxious at school. I'm always tired, and I don't get a good night's sleep. It's just endless."

Medications to manage attention deficit symptoms were a common topic among the study volunteers. They identified the varying effectiveness of taking stimulant medications. For example, Jason, who no longer took medication for ADHD, attributed some of his memory difficulties to stimulant medication. Roger built up a tolerance, so it lost its effectiveness to help him focus. Ben, who was highly distractible, stated that stimulant medication did help him to focus, but he wished that he could learn to cope without medication. He was saddened he was going to be burdened with managing his ADHD for life. All the participants claimed that they were compliant with taking antidepressants and antianxiety medications.

Confidence

With many elements competing for the participants' energy and attention such as anxiety, executive function difficulties, and past failures, it was not surprising that the participants struggled with self-doubt when attempting their studies. Robert's response was typical when he said, "I don't see myself as having a bunch of strengths, academically, as kind of proven by my track record." Yet every participant was working toward a degree and new successes were helping to fuel an emerging self-confidence. Robert began to build confidence when he was put on the Dean's List. "It contributed to giving me confidence that I was going to be able to do well, which in turn made me feel better. I had had so many unsuccessful academic experiences. It was reassuring to know I was doing well."

In connection to self, the participants related their experiences and insights regarding their understanding of their learning, which included a sense of their intelligence, memory, comorbid psychiatric disabilities, and confidence and the impact of these elements in producing academic work. With their abilities to connect with their inner lives, the participants were also clear about ways to connect with others.

Connection to Others

Being Seen

All participants identified their need to be seen, figuratively and concretely, and to be understood by others as fundamental to their success in college. Lisa wanted her professors to know her name without "having to look at a sheet with your face on it." It was frustrating and discouraging when this was not the case. Jason mentioned sitting in the middle of a classroom where he felt never seen. Consequently, he felt discouraged from asking questions. "If I had an issue, I'd never talk to anybody."

It was validating and encouraging when they experienced being seen in a class. Roger provided the example of a professor who built rapport, reporting that "I still talk to him. He gave me feedback on what I wrote, and he really wanted to open the conversation about where I should go with the writing. That was really cool to have someone actually take an interest."

Jane liked the idea of being seen by the other students in the class. She enrolled in a discussion-based writing class where everyone came to each class with a piece of writing. She was excited to report, "I read in this class! It was like they opened Pandora's box." The sense of being seen, which supported a feeling of safety, enabled Jane to explore her learning potential contained in her personal Pandora's box.

In some cases, when participants felt unseen, they failed or withdrew from courses. This was particularly problematic in large classes. Helen took a class with 150 other students. She stated:

> No one cared if you came to class. It was a lecture hall. I like to go to class, but if one day I'm not in the mood to go to class and no one's going to notice that I'm there? No. I won't be there.

"I really think that failing that class was what sent me over the edge," stated Lisa when relating her experience in a large class. "I felt like I don't want to be here anymore. I'm done!"

Not being seen meant lack of connection with fellow students and especially with professors. Participants felt uncared for because professors did not know their names and professors were unaware of their attendance. These factors made it difficult for students to self-advocate and made the participants feel isolated. When participants "felt supported" and were not "going it alone," they found success. Jason explained:

> I've experienced success for the first time. That I will acknowledge and am extremely happy about it. It wouldn't have happened if I wasn't involved in a program like this (academic support). Having someone to talk to and get some feedback, knowledgeable feedback back, turned into a pretty big plus. I always had so many problems with school. It turned into a big plus for me.

Relationships

Relationships were critical to academic success, according to the study participants. For example, relationships with their professors supported feeling understood and cared for, which connected to authentic support. When they felt understood, they felt supported. Increased interactions between the participants and their fellow classmates and between participants and their professors was important to their academic success because these interactions were evidence that students and professors appeared to care; these interactions provided the participants with feedback regarding their learning; and these interactions indicated that their contributions to the class were valued.

The impersonal nature of large classes contributed to the absence of relationship or connection with classmates and professors. Mike remembered a biology class of "435 students to be exact. It was one of those courses you take with a clicker. That was not a good scenario for me!" The evidence that smaller class size yielded success was consistent across all the participants. Helen stated, "If you go to class and spend the time in class, professors will help you more. They'll see that you go to class and there's a reason that you're struggling. It's like 'Okay, Helen comes to class every day; why didn't she do well on her paper?'" Helen felt that intellectual investment in large courses was the responsibility of the student rather than the professors. "If you're investing time in the course, the teacher should invest time in you, as well. I feel at big universities there's no connection between student and teacher when there should be because it's important."

The participants also stated that having individual rapport with professors encouraged them to invest more deeply in the learning process. Roger spoke of the value of:

> . . . someone who actually will come in and discuss things with you. Who actually will say, 'Hey Roger, what did you think of this?' I can come to a professor after class or before class with something I learned about the subject, or just talk in general as another human being. I find establishing a rapport helps greatly. Some professors are open to that; other professors really aren't. I find the ones who are make it much more enjoyable, much easier to get really enveloped in the work. For me it's really about the human connection.

Support

Authentic support allowed for freedom and shared power in the supportive relationship. When receiving academic support, participants described their experiences with control over the amount and type of support. Ben described his despair in not receiving real help that met his needs. Fully understanding his intellectual abilities, his frustration turned to hopelessness when considering the possibility to realize his talents, saying:

> It's not much support when you're complimented and people say, 'Oh you have no idea. You're brilliant.' I know that. I don't need to be told that a thousand times.

As much as I forget things, I remember that one! Let's not talk about potential. Let's talk about how fricking to change this. I don't care what my potential is if my potential can't be reached; I can't access it.

Robert described his current experiences with his academic support professor. He was able to discuss his foils in a nonjudgmental environment. When the Robert felt understood, he felt supported, reporting:

I don't want study tips. I just like having a safety net, and for me, Mary is that safety net. I can bounce anything off of her. It doesn't have to be something academic; it can be personal matters. She's awesome with that, and that's what I need as a student. I think she's a very accepting person. That's the biggest support I need. I've got some family up here and a few friends, but it's things I wouldn't talk to those people about anyway. There's a sense of confidentiality and comfort. I got that from the get-go, and that was encouraging. That's the biggest service provided. It's support. It's just support. Going to school. Going to classes. These things trip me up. I need someone I can fall back on, like when I start to lose confidence in myself, which happens periodically throughout a semester. I have had a bad past, so it's naïve to think that those things can't happen again. The ability to talk it out with Mary, and be like hey, 'I'm starting to slip right now. I haven't done anything this week.' She's the only person I've ever been able to tell that to.

I like that Mary didn't dictate what direction our sessions would go in. From the first semester she knew that I was older; knew that I was opinionated. From day one, we had a rapport that was easy. She knew what I wanted to do, and I knew what she was about. Talking to Mary helps me feel better. So, it helps me to do work because it lets me unload any stress and any anxiety I have about school. I still do not go to every single class or turn every assignment in on time. Those things I can talk to her about; it's just refreshing.

Robert appreciated that his support program had "dedicated people with dedicated time to dedicate to you." As Jason said, "You just hit a wall when you don't have support. It's a give-and-take kind of thing. Support is everything."

Professors

The participants valued professors who were flexible, had some understanding of ADHD, and were accessible after class. They preferred professors who invited questions and were able to "draw students in" and engage them in the class. "If you don't have people that draw students in, who else is going to do it?" asked Roger. He noted, "You can have the most interesting material in the world, but if you don't have an inviting person telling you what's going on with the material, you lost three-quarters of the class right there." Robert added, "I need answers, which is a strength, I guess. I like to bug my professors a little too much with asking questions. It's because I want to know more." Ben talked about a professor with whom he connected because he was flexible regarding assignment parameters and accessible outside of class. He said:

> My economics teacher was probably one of my favorite professors. He was one of the most understanding and flexible professors I have ever had. He was amazing. One time I emailed him because I had trouble with the final presentation. I asked him if he could meet with me outside of class. The class only met Wednesdays. I met with him on a Monday afternoon at lunchtime. He met me in the cafeteria. He totally didn't have to do that. He said, 'Just give it to me in the next couple days.' I ended up doing it that night.

Jane complained about professors who were inflexible about deadlines and criteria for assignment submissions, saying:

> You have to turn in the assignment on time, and you have to match the professor's criteria, not your own criteria. So, if you go above and beyond the call of duty, but you turn it in late, they're going to give you a D anyway.

Participants like Jason, for example, stated that it was important for professors to have some understanding of ADHD and learning disabilities:

If a student has ADD, and he's in your class, if you don't know how to help you can't help. Professors should be educated about identifying why a student's struggling. They should deal with that on a more one-on-one personal level. Just talk about it. At that point the students, I feel, are comfortable, number one, and feel they can talk to the professor.

Roger summed it up when he stated, "I know it's difficult, but honestly the reason I've gotten through the courses I've gotten through, is by getting to know the professor and working with the professor."

Accountability

Developing a rapport with professors provided opportunities for feedback, offered individualized support, and helped hold the participants accountable for their assignments. The students valued having someone with whom to be accountable, who knew them, and who did not judge them. The academic support professor was that person. Lisa asserted, "I think that there should be a person you have to check in with. I'm accountable for things when I come here." The ability to speak freely about the obstacles to beginning work, to sustaining effort to complete work, and to submitting work was one of the most highly valued part of the relationship with their professor. Jason stated clearly:

> When it comes to schoolwork, I have to have some accountability, and it can't be to myself. I believe in

guidance and learning how to cope with it yourself, but you need someone other than yourself that you're consistently accountable to. It can't be your parents either. I'm serious, because you can easily ignore your parents, and you can more than easily ignore yourself.

In a nonjudgmental, emotionally safe environment, participants were allowed the space to examine the obstacles to producing tangible work. In working to improve accountability, they explored ways to accomplish the difficult executive function tasks of self-activation, inhibiting desires to engage in immediately gratifying activities like Facebook, and sustaining effort to complete assignments. Robert was motivated to do this work. He said:

I didn't want to give myself excuses or avenues to get away from my academic responsibility. There's no point in lying about where I am anymore or where I stand. If you're not going to class, you're going to fail. Your advisor, your parents, your support professor, they're all going to know anyway. There's accountability in that.

Connection to the Work

Failure

Each study volunteer had endured painful school failures of all sorts. Reframing failure was important so that the participants could begin again. Withdrawing from college was a common event among them. There was always a tipping point: health, humiliation, lack of accommodations, and limited connections to others. Ben, the youngest in the study group, was in the process of considering transferring to another school. Jane had withdrawn and then re-enrolled in her current college. The remaining participants had attended multiple previous universities. Jane found failure when her depression interfered with her studies. "When I'm unsuccessful it's because I haven't attended class or I haven't turned in my work." Ben claimed,

"There's a million factors that tie into why I did not succeed in the proper timeline academically." He disclosed one of these reasons. "I stopped going to class. I would just get drunk with my friends, like three or four times a week. Seemed to be a lot of students doing that, but they were also going to class. I was not." Roger was refused testing accommodations in one of his major courses, stating:

> The professor refused to give me a separate location and extended time for the final. And then when the dean of students, who was in charge of disability services, emailed him, he never responded to the dean of students' emails. So, I had to take the final in a room with 100 other people. I ended up failing.

One semester, Jason experienced a health emergency, revealing, "I got sick during the beginning of a semester and failed a class. Those things really weigh on you, even if it is really out of your control. It's still a tick in the failure column, which is already the size of the Empire State

Building." While attending her first college, Lisa misunderstood the guidelines for one of her classes. Although she received "A" grades on all her written assignments, she did not attend the course classes. Consequently, her professor gave her an "F" as her final grade. Lisa took responsibility for her attendance, but failing the course changed her life. Lisa explained:

> All because I didn't attend class. That was the reason. When I look back now, I got straight A's in that class. Straight A's. Like fabulous writing. There were a lot of things going on in my life at that time, and that really was the last straw. I called my sister, and I told her, 'I did it. I'm done with school. I'm out!' It was a very pivotal moment.

Beginning Tasks

All the volunteers described difficulties with beginning academic tasks. Ben moaned, "Getting started is impossible. Impossible!" To treat this issue of self-activation strictly from an executive function frame was leaving something out. Absolutely, executive function was an important issue; however, creative process was possibly in play here, which was the need to be outwardly unproductive while inwardly taking time to work on ideas. This was often at the peril of meeting deadlines or neglecting other assignments. Outward, visible evidence of beginning or demonstrating that the student had begun an assignment was difficult because of both executive function and creative process. The participants described the process of taking extensive time in thinking and then executing assignments very quickly. Unfortunately, this meant missing deadlines or missing steps in assignment criteria. Jane described herself as "procrastination station." She continued, "I'm told I have a paper due. I'll write it in an hour or something, but it'll take me days to take that hour of my time to write it." Initiating visible academic work took time, but once the task began, the participants commonly stated that the work was completed quickly. Participants attributed the delay in initiating the demonstration of academic work to needing time to think about the work, slow processing in order to thoroughly consider the assignment, avoidance of academic tasks that were unengaging or that triggered perfectionism, and distractions such as Facebook.

Mike described the difficulty of self-activation, but once involved, produced "good work on paper," only to be thwarted by submission requirements such as formatting. He said:

> It's premiere executive functioning. Can't get started; can't complete each step of a process. You get a list of ten things to do. You do eight and think, 'I totally nailed it.' But the nineth and tenth step might be to turn in the paper on time and have a certain formatting style that the professor really wants. So, all of all of a sudden, your paper is basically useless because you didn't follow the formatting, and you didn't turn it in on time. But that's where it is. Even if you do 90 percent or 80 percent of the steps really well, like the

research, the presentation, the working with groups, you fall apart in the end and then it's the slide.

These adult students were vulnerable to "the slide." They were often functioning close to their tipping points. A late paper could potentially trigger an old pattern of behavior that could sabotage successful course completion.

Attention

Each participant had a diagnosis of ADHD, so each complained about attention difficulties regarding distractibility and the effects that problems with sustained attention had on school work production, reading and listening comprehension, memory, organization, and disposition. Ben was extremely frustrated with his own inability to sustain attention when attempting independent studying, saying, "If I'm reading a chapter in a textbook, more times than not, I'll end up with my eyes on a word, but I won't even know what's on the page. I'll have to reread." Roger also had trouble staying with assignments. The energy it took to stay focused depleted his will to work towards completion. He commented, "Staying on task can be hard. Once I do start something, there are times my focus peters out pretty fast because I do get tired." Sustained effort was problematic if an assignment was uninteresting or when perfectionism played a role. Helen stated, "With a couple of my projects, if it didn't turn out exactly how I wanted it to be, and it was probably really close, I lost all drive to do it."

The effort to retrieve oneself repeatedly from both internal and external distraction competed with strong abilities to comprehend coursework and complete assignments. Mike joked, "I gotta see what's going on. I sort of feel like my dog. Every time the door opens, I'm like, 'Who was that?'" Mike identified a strategy he used to balance internal and external distractions when studying, commenting, "I always play talk radio. It's noise in the background that I can control. I can control the volume. It's white noise." For several of the participants, lecture style classes were particularly challenging. Both internal thoughts and environmental distractions took attention away from the lecturer. Jason simply said, "It's like being asleep with your eyes open. You're there, but you're not. Then you catch yourself, 'Oh, what's he talking about now?' That happens to me quite often." Lisa complained:

> It's the sitting that I'm not very good at. There's too much information in my head. There's no room for anything else. I think about everything else possible while I'm in class. I'm thinking about a thousand other things than what's actually going on.

Roger explained that lectures often trigger internal thinking:

> If the professor is moderately engaging, my mind will still wander. One word of the lecture will trigger me to think about something else. I'll go daydream about

whatever that word triggered me to think about. Just tangents. Tangents all the time.

Creativity

The volunteers described a need for a sense of timelessness. It was thought-provoking to compare the internal process of creativity with difficulties of executive function: the outward appearance of low productivity when engaged in deep states of concentration; the outward appearance of procrastination before energy was available to execute ideas; and missed deadlines because attention dedicated exclusively to an idea was an attribute of creativity and executive function difficulties. In either case, the need to experience a sense of timelessness was important for the well-being of these participants and for optimal satisfaction in learning and creative production.

All of the study participants described a mental process of creativity that involved a protracted time of outward unproductiveness. Roger described this mental activity as a "trance-like state." He continued, "I almost kind of black out when I get in the middle of a paper. By the end of it, I don't really know what I've written until I've gone back over it." Mike stated, "You can get lost in your own writing and your own thinking." The volunteers needed time to devote to their thinking and then the ideas materialized seemingly spontaneously. Jane explained:

> I have to let my gears spin for a while. I won't write at all for a long period of time. I'll have all these ideas

spinning and spinning, a lot of stuff floating around in the stew. I just have to wait for that crockpot to ding. Then I'll get a lot done in a short period of time.

Jane also played piano and painted and said that the same process occurred in both. Jason also required ample time before showing any outward production, adding, "An idea would come in my head, and I'd just think about it for days. I wouldn't have drawn anything yet. Literally, I would be drawing a picture in my head over time."

Once Mike was able to lock into his writing, he found the work to be very satisfying:

> As soon as I get started, once I get rolling, I can put good work on paper. I've been known to write for six straight hours; just putting pen to paper; fingers on the keyboard; and really hammer out good work. Once I break the ice, I tend to zone in. It has to be something I enjoy, obviously, for it to keep my focus, but then I do good work. If it's engaging, it's worth it.

The participants also all agreed that time dedicated to the execution of their ideas consumed their thinking, often to the exclusion of all else. Lisa related:

> All my force goes into it. If I'm doing something, I'm doing it well, and I like it, that will be the only thing I touch. That will be all I can think about, all I can do. If I'm making a painting or something like that, I can't pay attention to anything else until it's completed. It's

like my house right now even. An absolute disaster. I've got to follow it until it doesn't have my attention anymore.

Participants reported the ability to make "connections between seemingly disparate ideas." As Mike said:

> I have the ability to make a logical jump. I might have two subjects that might not seem like they're linear. I have the ability to make that next jump of logic and tie them together. If you have creativity, you can make that logical jump. You can join them together, whether they're topics in a paper or questions on a test. You can relate them with creativity.

When discussing their actual work in the arts, the participants described the "torture" of perfectionism, which conflicted with the need for fast results and gratification. Jane disclosed, "My creativity is kind of a miserable thing. It's painful and brutal. I don't know how I get anything done." Jason, a risktaker, who "never follows the rules," truly suffered:

> You're always trying to push yourself and push yourself and push yourself. I'd get to this point where I'd try to seek perfection, and it would be right in front of me. I never hit it. It's one of those things that tortures you. There is a quote that a finished piece of art is just art that's abandoned. You're never finished.

Lisa talked about the ways she managed her perfectionism:

> I usually do things more in pen or charcoal; something where I can't erase. Painting, too. I can't erase a painting. It's just very straightforward… I like quickness. I like to be able to see the end near. That's why I prefer drawing, I think."

Helen needed time to think through a creative project and at the same time was frustrated that this mental process slowed her down. Her desire to execute a perfect project also conspired to slow her down. On the other hand, Helen also knew that eventually the mental work would come together and she would feel inspired to be outwardly productive. Helen explained:

> When I'm trying to be creative or do a project, I definitely have to slow down, because I want it to be perfect. I don't want to have to do it over, because then I get discouraged. If I want it to be perfect then I have to wait awhile and think it through. I try to think of exactly what I want it to look like. It seems like I'm putting it off, but actually, I'm working on it.

Engagement

All the data was repeated in the engagement category. All of the above contributed to engagement in learning. Despite the complexities of having ADHD, such as executive function difficulties and mental health challenges, there was a strong desire on the part of the interviewees to engage in deeps ways with their college learning experiences. Because they were exceptionally curious, these participants asked many questions in class. "I definitely have a thousand more questions than everybody else," said Lisa. "If it's something that I want to learn about, something that I need to know, I want to know, then I will do anything in my power to learn everything I need to learn," she asserted. Roger also articulated the joy of learning:

> Interestingly enough, I do really like learning. It's funny how that happens. The act of acquiring knowledge makes me happy, so that's one thing that keeps me going back to schoolwork. My natural state is curious. Being able to do new things with what I know now is always a very fun concept. Being able… feeling more enabled, more empowered to do things because of what I've learned. I do have the habit of going very deep into what I'm learning. I will learn many layers of it, and absorb as much of it as I possibly can. And it takes a while.

Recommendations for Teaching Practice

The participants offered two concrete recommendations for teaching practice. First, participants suggested explicitly framing assignments as a continuation of class conversations and interactions, which utilized texts and research.

Framing academic activity as ongoing would help with self-activation in initiating independent work. Secondly, participants stated that they needed clarity from professors when assigning work. When assignments were too open-ended, they felt compelled to create something innovative, which required extensive time and energy.

In broader conceptual terms, the following suggestions were presented:

- Foster creative work as a means of self-reflection, to support self-understanding as a bridge to students' compassion for themselves as learners.
- Enable students to realize that creative abilities are critical to connecting to academic work and experiencing academic success.
- Assist students in realizing the value of their creative strengths.
- Conceptualize the creative process as valuable way to navigate academic tasks.

It was important to emphasize connections between students and professors for support, stimulation, and feedback; the similarities between executive function difficulties and aspects of creative processes; and the need for building space for inward productivity. Gnezda's (2015) explanation of the creative process in terms of cognitive arousal when engaged in deep thinking and in the moments of activation to execute a creative idea was potentially informative when considering teaching practices. Lowered arousal during deep thinking and then heightened arousal during production resided with present differences in executive functioning. From the participants' perspective, the creative process was exciting and intrinsically rewarding. Unfortunately, it often conflicted with the external structures of traditional academics. The volunteers indicated that realistically they needed to reconcile their desire to experience a sense of timelessness with inhabiting a time-bound academic world. They wished for enough time for the creative process. In the context of academic external structures, it was important to help students explore opportunities to experience a sense of timelessness, which facilitated deep engagement, gratifying learning, and valuable products resulting from their efforts.

Summary

A small group of adult college students with superior cognitive strengths, creative abilities, and ADHD initiated this qualitative research project. They wanted to explore their learning strengths and challenges; share their understanding of their learning with a larger college community; and offer teaching practice recommendations that might better address their learning needs. It was interesting to note that the participants highly valued "human connection" as essential to academic success and engagement. Rapport and especially relationships with professors who were personally interested in them, with whom they felt they could discuss difficulties, and with whom they felt understood stimulated, enabled the participants to sustain engagement in learning. It was also thought-provoking to compare the internal process of creativity with an ADHD characteristic of hyper-focusing: the outward appearance of low productivity when engaged in deep states of concentration; the outward appearance of procrastination before the energy is available to execute ideas; and missed deadlines because attention is dedicated exclusively to the idea. In either case, the need to experience a sense of timelessness was important for the well-being of these participants and for optimal satisfaction in learning and creative production.

The adult college students who participated in this study had a history of struggling to make academic progress because creative processes were incompatible with traditional academic structures. Highly self-reflective, these participants articulated strong needs for connection with others in order to stimulate intellectual connections, which stimulated deep engagement in the curricula. When involved in academic pursuits, the volunteers stated that they had many questions. More questions made work production take longer because more complex processes were in place, including the issues of having ADHD and the coexisting difficulties that are part of ADHD. Authentic academic support enabled them to navigate college academic learning structures and discover satisfying learning experiences. Deep engagement in learning involved the interactions among connection to self, others, and the work.

CHAPTER 4

KNOW ME: LIVED EXPERIENCES OF ADULT COLLEGE STUDENTS WITH ADHD AND COEXISTING PSYCHIATRIC DISORDERS

Jeremy's Perspective

I HAVE ATTENTION DEFICIT disorder. I have, obviously, Tourette's Syndrome. I always forget to say that because it's so glaringly obvious. And, I suffer from clinical depression and bipolar disorder, which means I have the hypo-manic episodes. It's not like fly to Vegas and spend ten grand. It's kind of get peppy and maybe lose my filter a little bit and act erratic rather than grand crazy things. So, I have some episodes of hypo-mania, but more often I have the troughs rather than the peaks. Instead of having really high peaks, my disorder is more characterized by an abrupt switch between the two.

If I have a bad day with Tourette's, I just have more tics. I'm louder and I move more. It's strenuous on my body, and it's distracting to me because I'm literally being jarred away from what I'm trying to do. But that's not as bad as if I feel differently than I want to feel. My whole emotional state is different from where I expect to be. It's weird when I think I'm going to react one way and then my visceral reaction's something entirely different. My neurochemistry is dictating something that I don't want. I said visceral reaction on purpose, because it's not my logical reaction. It's literally what I'm feeling in my chest. I can think what I want, regardless. It's nothing to do with what I feel. I can be logical and still have these awful mood swings. The worst part is when I recognize my logical thoughts and then the anxious or angry or scared thoughts go in there, I'm like, "Aww crap. Get that out of there. I'm trying to pay attention to the real thoughts!" What most people don't realize is that each tic is a thought. I know what tic is going to happen before it happens because I feel it, for lack of a better word. I think it before I do it. Often, I feel it in the part of the body or the voice that it's going to happen. So, it's brain activity before it's physical or vocal activity. Not only do I have intrusive thoughts because of bipolar, depression, and attention deficit, I have extra brain activity because of the tics. Sometimes it's like Grand Central Station on Friday night at 5:00.

I'm like an Italian sportscar. I am built to be as good as someone could possibly be for a very brief amount of time, and then I break down entirely. We're kindred spirits! It would work beautifully and make wonderful noise and drive impeccably, and then all of sudden it would billow smoke and sputter, and then it would just blow up. Story of my life. I'm functioning great, I'm singing music perfectly, I'm writing these great stories, I'm taking care of everything I need to do in my life, and then oh man, I feel like shit! Why am I so angry all the time? Oh, she doesn't like me. I have so much I got to do, and end up on the couch for a week.

Introduction

Adult college students with co-existing attention deficits and psychiatric disorders present unique and complex learning needs and challenges to colleges. Students enrolled in the Adult Center, a college academic support program, also encounter limited understanding of their needs by others in a college community. As indicated in Chapter Three, these students have histories of inconsistent academic performance and difficulties progressing towards degree completion. Most of them have withdrawn from multiple colleges and universities.

Several students enrolled in the Adult Center were frustrated by their experiences with their college community. In addition to one-to-one work, I met weekly with adult students as a group. It was in this group that students expressed a desire to conduct a formal study to help people on the institutional side understand mental illness and, they hoped, with increased understanding from the college, they would get their academic needs met. Together, the students and I designed a qualitative study to deepen the understanding of the learning needs of these adult college students with co-occurring attention deficits and mental health challenges; provide a space for adult student voices to describe their lived experiences as learners; identify from the students' point of view academic practices and supports that met their needs; and contribute to the academic literature addressing adult college students with co-occurring attention deficits and mental health difficulties.

Brief Literature Review

Based on their research, Brown (2017, 2013) and Barkley (2015) state that the DSM-V describes *Attention Deficit Disorders* (ADHD) two dimensionally as challenges of focus or sustained attention and/or significant difficulties of hyperactivity or impulsivity. Both argue that a central feature of ADHD is the limited ability to regulate emotions. People with ADHD have challenges with working memory in that it is problematic to hold the characteristics of a situation, which elicit emotional responses long enough to evaluate and execute modulated or appropriate responses to the situation.

Inadequate working memory causes a person with ADHD to insufficiently attend to the multiple emotions that play a critical role in guiding thought and behavior, or those emotions become eclipsed by one specific emotion in a way that doesn't adequately take other relevant emotion-connected thoughts into account (Brown, 2014, p. 37).

Often a single emotion can overwhelm an individual with ADHD to the point that thinking through a situation to produce an appropriate emotional response is distorted. Frequently, the response is impulsive or a display of frustration and anger followed by embarrassment and shame. Since individuals with ADHD are vulnerable to their own emotions, it may not be surprising that they often live with comorbid or co-existing psychiatric disorders.

According to Barkley (2015, 2022), 80% of individuals with ADHD are at risk for one additional psychiatric disorder; 50% are liable for two other psychiatric disorders; and 33% of this population experiences three or more psychiatric disorders. Major depressive disorder (MDD), dysthymia, anxiety disorders, substance use disorder (SUD), and oppositional defiant disorder (ODD), are most commonly comorbid with attention deficits (Barkley, 2015; Antshel & Barley, 2011). Brown (2017) states that adults with ADHD have six times the likelihood of having at least one other psychiatric disorder that needs diagnosis and treatment in the adult's lifetime. Brown further states that the reason for increased incidents of comorbid psychiatric disorders is the result of the underlying executive function disorder, making these adults more vulnerable to additional psychiatric challenges. Executive function impairments play a role in anxiety, where individuals have difficulty shifting attention to larger aspects of environmental cues and, instead, focus narrowly on perceived threats and hyper-focus on those threats.

Challenges to working memory make it difficult to retain relevant information from the environment while considering more limited information in the larger context and therefore determine an appropriate response to the perceived threat. The same appears to be true for adults with ADHD who have comorbid depression. The impaired ability to retain multiple pieces of information and weigh triggers for depression in a larger context makes it difficult to regulate depressive emotions. Several studies now confirm the co-morbidity of additional psychiatric disorders in adults with ADHD (Joshi & Wozniak, 2015; Krone & Newcorn, 2015; Pliszka, 2015; Prince, 2015; Wilens & Morrison, 2015). Joshi and Wozniak add bipolar disorders to the list. Brown (2013) describes the overlap of ADHD and bipolar disorder as the inability to regulate emotions or levels of arousal.

The Study

The students and I decided that the best approach to giving voice to their lived experiences in a college environment in order to articulate their learning needs and inform the larger college community was through qualitative interviews. We followed the protocols for a formal qualitative research study, which included IRB approval, Letters of Informed Consent, and assurances of anonymity.

Seven students volunteered to interview individually with me. Of the seven volunteers, four were women and three were men whose ages ranged from 22 to 38 years. One participant was a graduate student and the others were part-time or full-time undergraduates. As measured by the *Weschler Adult Intelligence Scale-Fourth Edition* (WAIS-IV), each participant had scores greater than 120 on the Verbal Comprehension Index and/or the Performance Index. They each had documented diagnoses of ADHD and comorbid psychiatric disorders, which included bipolar disorder, major depressive disorder (MDD), generalized anxiety disorder (GAD), obsessive-compulsive disorder (OCD), post-traumatic stress disorder PTSD), and Tourette Syndrome.

Results

Of the 33 original codes that came from the transcriptions, 15 second-tiered categories emerged from the data. Although presented here in a linear manner, these categories were interrelated. They clustered under three final categories; internal experiences, external experiences, and internal and external experiences.

Internal Experiences

Internal experiences meant the ways in which each individual participant experienced their ADHD and mental health challenges. Six main topics emerged from the interviews regarding their internal lives. They were: sleep, exhaustion, stress, control, executive function, and struggles. None of the categories were discrete; they were interrelated.

Sleep

Sleep challenges were common among all the participants. Sleep onset and sustained sleep are often problematic among people with ADHD; however, coupled with episodes of depression, created extensive challenges for the study volunteers. During these episodes, several participants disclosed that problems with sleep often translated to remaining in bed for prolonged periods of time. James shared his reflections about time spent in bed:

> Depression has had actually a bigger impact than the ADHD just because of how I've ebbed and flowed for years. I go through cycles. Most of my childhood and adolescence was steeped in depression. So, it's what I got used to. It was a very comforting thing because I could control everything. Even though it wasn't exciting or exhilarating or anything productive, I had complete control over my environment. I was very secluded, very isolated, and that sense of control brought such a relief. It was a sense of solace, like I had the power to manipulate the variables that were around me. Even though there were very few, it was the perception that I had control. It was very easy to return to that because I was so used to the emotions. I knew exactly what to expect. Being in a depressive, isolated state was a great way to avoid everything. My days were very constant sitting in bed. There were not many variables that were going to change, and what they were, I could have good control over them. So why would I pass that up? That seems like a really good offer. The fine print, though, is what got me.

In general, people go to bed to reduce stimulation in order to recover from the stimulation of the day. When James experienced a depressive episode, he went to bed to manage overwhelming stimulation.

Exhaustion

Susan spoke for everyone when she described navigating her daily life. "It's exhausting. It's exhausting!" With managing ADHD and coexisting mental health difficulties while getting less than optimal rest, it was not surprising that the participants cited exhaustion as an ongoing experience. Brittany coined the phrase, "strategic use of energy" when she talked about the complexity of living with bipolar disorder as a student and having enough energy to meet the requirements of academics. She noted:

> The nature of bipolar disorder is I never know how I'm going to feel each day. Basically, the nature of my life is really unpredictable. It gets scary when I have a lot of work because there are times when I can handle it, and then I'm like okay, 'Can I keep up this I-can-handle-it mentality?' Probably not. I just never know when I'm not going to be able to write a paper and when I am. I'm a history major, so I have to write a lot and I have to read a lot. Sometimes I sit down and just physically can't write a paper. In the fall, I deal with some depression and also some anxiety, and sometimes I just don't have any energy at all to do anything. In the spring, I mainly deal with mania, or hypomania. I deal with anxiety on top of that. So, it's hard to write. And sometimes my professors view that as slacking. They're like, 'Why didn't you start earlier?' I'm sorry. Yesterday I was fine, but I didn't know that today I wasn't going to be fine. It's complicated. Sometimes I just can't get my work done.

James described his process for determining his strategic use of energy:

> I have to assess where this problem is coming from. Is it a variable that I can control, or is it a variable I can't control? The problem is already there, so I determine whether or not I'm going to even allocate effort to this. If it's within my control, I definitely consider going through the whole listing out if this is worth my energy. It's really more of weighing pros and cons; how much energy to expend; what am I going to get in return from this? But, if it's outside my sphere of influence, I try not to concern myself, because that's just a waste of energy.

Managing symptoms of both ADHD and mental illness while meeting the demands of a student was a daunting assignment for these participants.

Stress

Sleep problems, exhaustion from managing symptoms of ADHD and mental illness, and energy expended to focus on academic requirements generated high levels of stress in all the participants. Brittany explained, "Life is really stressful for me. I feel more stress than other people because I'm really sensitive. My sensitivity gets worse with hypomania." Emma described the circular nature of control, fatigue and stress; each contributing to the other:

> I'm so tired when I get really in a hole, not because I'm trying to avoid. It's because I'm controlling. I'm using so much energy to control my stress and not think about it, and keep the lid on it, and keep the scary in a box that I'm just exhausted.

Nina elaborated further on the contributors to her stress. These negatively affected enjoying her studies and the quality of her life:

> I feel I am not enjoying what I am learning because I keep thinking about the results. I am not relaxed in the class. I even lose what I am learning because I am thinking, 'How can I write the papers?' Then I go home and I am stressed. That affects my relationship with my kids, with my husband. Because I focus on academic work, that takes me from the social life with my kids and my family. And, to be able to focus on my academics, to put in energy for writing, I can't do my field work because there's no time and space.

Control

The participants found it a daily challenge to stay in control of the many moving parts of their lives. As suggested in previous sections, they frequently felt overwhelmed. Jeremy stated, "It's like Grand Central Station on Friday night at five o'clock!" Chris was easily overwhelmed because his bipolar disorder was difficult to treat. He noted:

My mania. It's almost like I'm trapped inside myself. I don't have control over what I'm doing. I can't think or process it, because I'm not in the right mental frame of mind. If I have an episode, whether it's manic or depressive, I'm going to need to be hospitalized probably, if it's really, really bad. Usually, I can forget about that semester. I can forget about those courses. I have to drop them. I have a lot of "W"s (course withdrawals) over my college career because of my mental health getting in the way. Sometimes it wasn't going to the hospital. Sometimes I just couldn't handle the courses. I had to drop half of them just to take the load off.

Jeremy also stated:

I hesitate to use the word 'control' because control suggests that there's a direct connection. I have control over circumstances such as how I eat, how I sleep, things that can set me up to have a better day. I can't just say, 'Okay, let's be calm.' I can't just make myself be immediately rational and even. That's not exactly possible. The term 'just do it,' like Nike, 'just do it,' yeah, no, that doesn't happen. That doesn't exist in my world.

Over the years working toward her college degree, Susan had acquired and practiced daily strategies that enabled her to be in control of her bipolar disorder. She reported:

It's not easy; it really has never been easy; and I don't expect it to ever just magically become easy. There is no magic pill. It's a work in progress every day, and that's why the tools that I have, the skills that I've amassed, I have to keep using them. I definitely have my routine where my alarm goes off, and I absolutely do not snooze it. Because if I snooze it, I'm never getting up. I take my meds. I have my med minder that has my morning and night all laid out. And I eat. I usually try to pick out my clothes the night before so I'm not just standing there wondering what I want to wear. I make sure that my basic self-care is done.

Susan continued:

I still will let some things pile up so high that it just becomes overwhelming, whether it's laundry or dishes or assignments. I used to be like, 'Yup, it's over. I'm done. Tapping out.' And I know that that's not an option for me anymore. I need to keep going, and the only way that I can keep going is little by little deal with the things that I've let pile up. Give myself the little wins.

Jeremy also wrestled daily to manage the complexities ADHD and multiple mental health difficulties. He contributed:

Most people would say I'm a full-time student. Really, I'm a part-time student; taking care of myself is a full-time job. There are an infinite number of things that can go wrong in a day, and when things do go wrong, it's often multiple small things that add up to some qualitative change in my daily habits that then affect my mood, which then affects my productivity and outward disposition. Waking up isn't a simple matter. Going to bed isn't a simple matter. Making sure I'm alert enough to do any given task is not a simple matter. Making sure I believe in myself to do a task is not a simple matter. We always talk about writing. While writing is one of my strengths, at the same time it's one of the things that's scariest for me because in order to really engage in the creative process, there's a loss of control there. Surrendering to that place of flow represents an unknown. I can disappear for awhile, and when I show back up there's things on the page. Sometimes it's scary to think of what might happen if I disappear for a little bit.

All the participants worked hard to maintain a delicate balance between taking care of themselves and taking on the burdens of academics.

Executive Function

The participants' main concerns regarding executive functioning were weaknesses in working memory and self-activation, which influenced organization and sustained attention. "My working memory is so impacted by my disability. That's not really something that's understood by the college. I think with most bipolar people their working memory is heavily impacted in a negative way," declared Brittany. "During my manic episodes, I can't be productive because I just can't get everything on paper or organized and I get irritated."

Emma described her own frustration:

> On the tests I get As, I talk in class, I understand. But turning in the stuff, and regularly turning in the stuff, is the hardest thing in the world because it's boring and slow to do. Writing is really slow. I know what I want to say. I just wish I could pick up my brain and rub it on the page and have it be done. Just squeeze. Okay, we're good! But it takes forever to get the sentences out.

James preferred highly engaging homework assignments and constant stimulation in class and in order to initiate tasks and sustain focus:

> I prefer having information constantly thrown at me. I like the more macro concepts of everything. As long as ideas and information are constantly fed to me, it keeps my mind active and engaged. Classes that are intellectual and the discussions are engaging, I tend to thrive. The classes that have lulls in them, or there's a lot more time given to explanations, is where I find myself drifting off in some reverie, somewhere far off, and I start losing focus of the class. Then I lack the motivation to initiate assignments, which obviously ends up in being procrastination.

When expressing his frustration with the interference of his executive function difficulties,

Jeremy emphasized, "If I could just do it, I would!"

Struggles

The participants related their many internal struggles as they navigated their academic lives. Some of the volunteers used words like "hard" and "scary" to describe their experiences. The previously discussed issues contributed to their challenges. Brittany stated, "If you're depressed, if you're manic and you can't organize your work, you can't perform in class that day." Susan asserted, "I'm already playing against a stacked deck. It's hard."

Nina described a time when the struggle almost got the better of her:

> It was hard. I remember crying, 'I'm done!' like a kid having a tantrum after school. When I finished my classes, I walked to the train, and just cried, cried, cried, cried. I didn't want to go back to school, but I had to go back. I cried, cried, cried and then I said, 'Okay, let's go. Let's do it.'

James offered his hopeful position:

> I believe that the mind is by far the strongest element and factor in any decision and anything regarding actual physical health, mental, or psychological. If you can keep convincing yourself that things are true, keep telling yourself, you'll eventually believe it's true. Even though there's very real chemical imbalances, our

minds can make ourselves do incredible things. I'm not saying it's going to be easy; it's hard. But it's not unmanageable. I realize as much as I am struggling, there are ways I know how to cope, and I can use effective mechanisms to succeed. Having convinced myself that I am capable, which definitely helps in the process of conquering the obstacles that I'm faced with.

External Experiences

The study participants shared their feelings about having mental illness in the context of the academic environment. People, professors, and support were three categories the volunteers discussed most in their interviews.

People

Excluding professors, the people to whom the participants referred were all those they encountered in the college community. Because of his mental illness, Chris frequently worried about others' perceptions of him as a competent student. He strongly stated:

> The stigma. Stigma in relation to mental health. I don't want anyone to think I can't do the work or to treat me differently. I want to be treated the same as everyone else. The main thing that needs to be done is to break down the stigma. Obliterate it!

Emma was reluctant to disclose her difficulties to others because she anticipated negative treatment:

> I don't like talking about it because I don't know the reaction I'm going to get from people. The small percentage of people who will be either empathetic or even have an inkling of what it's like, is just nonexistent. The possibility of oh-so-many-other annoying or just mean comments, I don't want to deal with. There's a huge risk in talking about it. People don't understand.

Nina was very anxious about interacting with her classmates in her doctoral program:

> I avoided talking with people, and I avoided any extracurriculars after my classes. I had this barrier because of my self-esteem. I felt like I was not good enough to be with these people. I told myself, 'It's okay to go home and escape.'

Brittany had difficulty reconciling her bipolar symptoms with the expectations of a college community. She also experienced the stigma of having a mental health disorder, which she understood to be based on limited understanding:

> In college they expect you to be predictable and to do your work and to meet deadlines. People like dependable and predictable people, and I'm not one of them. It's scary when they don't understand why I'm not pre-

dictable and dependable. They can't relate to that. The moment you talk about it, people just don't know what to do; they don't know how to handle it. There's a lack of education about mental illness. I think in a lot of colleges there's a culture of you hide it. I have to say from my experience, it's not a welcoming environment to be in college with a mental illness.

James talked about the responses he received from fellow students when he mentioned he had mental health challenges:

It's still taboo to talk about mental illness. I went to psychologists my entire life; I still go to one. When I brought it up to friends, I'm like, 'Oh I'm going to go see my psychologist,' as a regular thing. My friends were like, 'What do you mean? Why do you need to go to a psychologist?' For the first time I thought, 'Well, don't you go to one? I go to one. It's not a big deal.' I just thought that was a normal thing. I think part of the problem is that people aren't willing to speak out and say, 'Here's my problem; here's where I struggle; here's where you can help me,' because of the fear, the dread of being shunned by the community that they're involved with, for being different or not being able.

Even though now I know I'm definitely the outlier of the group, it doesn't really change my perspective. I couldn't honestly care less what other people think.

I know what I'm doing is helping me and that's what matters.

Susan also talked about the limited understanding she met on campus:

I really want people to understand that it's okay that they can't understand. It's okay that they can't fathom how deep my depression is. It's okay that they can't follow my 80-mile-an-hour thought speed. But it's not okay to discriminate against me because you don't understand. It's okay not to understand, but you have to include me, and you have to treat me as if I'm just another student.

Professors

It was not surprising that the participants had much to say about professors. Brittany struggled against the attitudes of some of her professors:

You're misunderstood for why you're not doing well. The professors see it as you're slacking because they're not educated about bipolar disorder. They think you don't care, and you don't want to be in school. I need people to know that my intentions are right.

I want to know that my professors value me. To know that I'm on the same page as someone is all I really need.

PERSPECTIVES ON ACADEMIC SUPPORT

Jeremy approached his professors at the start of each semester to disclose his disabilities:

> I always make it a point to talk to the professor on the first day to let them know what I'm like. But that does get tiring. Some professors are clearly disconcerted when I come out and tell them. They say, "Oh… okay," having that kind of cagey look in their eyes. They just don't know what to make of it.

James insisted on having a meeting with each of his professors about his disabilities:

> I feel like you should at least have to have ten to fifteen minutes to talk to the professor. That way you could explain in some sensitive detail in a more personal, intimate setting about what you struggle with and that way they're aware of the flaws that may occur throughout the semester.

Susan was very deliberate in her interactions with her professors:

> My relationships with my professors have benefitted from openness. I'm very open and honest with them about how I am; why I'm the way I am; and what they can do to not only help me, but help them with the rest of the class, because sometimes in the past I have overpowered the class. I feel like I really made some

great relationships with different professors that I know I can call on, even in years to come.

Support

There was an appreciation among the study participants for support that addressed their individual needs. They felt particularly supported when professors offered flexibility with assigned work and when faculty took an interest in them as individuals. For example, Nina excelled in a class where the professor encouraged her intellectual growth rather than emphasizing hard deadlines.

> I had a great professor who always supported me. That helped me to be relaxed in the class. He always said, 'You can do it. Look, it's not a big deal.' These words helped me. I enjoyed being in his classes. I also had open communication with him. If I needed something or I struggled and was anxious, I sent him email. 'Oh, can I have an extension?' and he would say, 'Yes.' I felt relaxed because I had this time, and I finished before the time.

Brittany valued the support she received from a faculty member who invested time to get to know her.

> I think one of the most important things I'm realizing is it's really nice to have an ally. Someone who sees you a couple of times a week and knows how you're doing.

Who isn't super judgmental and helps with the basic things to keep you on track. When you feel like you're going through college alone, it's miserable. I like to know that I have a few people who are in my corner and have the time of day for me, for me to come in and talk when I need something. That is very helpful. If I'm having a bad day, they can say, 'It's okay. It's not a big deal. We just keep going.'

It was interesting to note that the participants did not look for extraordinary accommodations. When they felt cared for, they felt supported.

Internal and External Experiences

The participants elaborated on subjects that were both intimate experiences and experiences in the context of being with others. The six main topics common among all the volunteers were: fear, isolation, depression, learning, progress, and change.

Fear

Internally, Jeremy feared losing control of keeping in check his multiple symptoms of his mental health disorders. Externally, he had to deal with other people's reactions to the visible manifestations of these disorders. Jeremy gave examples of these experiences:

I have disorders that generally promote disarray. Attention deficit, you're thinking all over the place. Manic depression, your mood's all over the place. Depression, you just kind of sink. And Tourette's, my sounds, words and actions are erratic and all over the place. Well, to an extent. They kind of clip in and out, and obviously, I can have a conversation. Since all of my disorders generally promote disarray, my tendency is to clamp down really hard on everything and try and bring them back in. So, when something requires letting go or easing into it and just opening up, that's one of the scariest propositions that could be made.

And it's not that I don't always trust myself. It's that I fear other people don't trust me. I've been continuously told or at least shown that I'm scary. I don't think I'm scary, but other people think I'm scary.

Emma continued to try to come to terms with her mental health difficulties. She worried, "It has been this big dark scary thing for so long; like, I'm broken in a way I don't know how to deal with." While she wrestled with her fears, she still had to disclose to professors every semester and anticipate inconsistent results. Emma related:

It's so terrifying to talk to my professors that way. To sit down and say, 'Look this is what's going on. This is what I'll be struggling with this semester.' I don't know if they'd understand. I don't know if it would make any difference.

Susan had a similar worry about disclosure:

> Whenever I have needed to approach a professor about extra time or an extension or leniency due to my mental illness, I'm always very nervous. It doesn't matter if I've known the professor, if we have a good relationship, I'm always nervous. If I've asked them before, I feel like they might just be like, 'Oh, this again.'

Susan offered a quote that helped her when she felt fearful of her internal experiences and fearful of other people. She shared:

> I saw this quote today, and it says, 'You don't always have to be strong, but you do have to be brave.' I think the biggest thing is that when I can't be strong, I have to be brave because I'm going to get that backlash from other people who just don't get it. I'm going to get that backlash from myself.

Isolation

Feeling isolated and being isolated were frequent realities among the participants. For Brittany, fear and isolation were integrated, one influencing the other.

> I'm on my own most of the time, and it's scary. Sometimes I just can't get my work done. And it's hard, because my friends in college don't know how to handle

it. So, it's like you just feel alone and scared. It escalates to a certain point where I just can't do my work at all.

Chris had a history of rejection and bullying. In order to protect himself from future painful experiences on a college campus, he chose to isolate from his classmates. Chris stated, "Just going to class and then going home was better for me because I wouldn't be open to scrutiny from other students." Susan stated that feeling isolated and being isolated by others contributed to episodes of mental illness:

> You can't see your worth, and that'll get lost. That leads down a very dark road, especially when all those negativities are coming at you and especially when it's coming from yourself. With mental illness, nobody is going to be harder on yourself than you.

Even though I know that I'm not the only one on this campus with mental health issues, and even though I know some of the people who are also struggling, sometimes I feel very alone. It doesn't matter that you know who else is struggling or that other people are struggling. They're not you, and they're not in that moment with you. So, sometimes it's just very alone.

Depression

Of the psychiatric disorders coexisting with ADHD, depression was the most common among the study volunteers. Emma expressed her frustration with the unpredictable nature of her depression and ways that it interfered with her academics and her ability to obtain accommodations. Emma explained:

> With depression, it's a constant, constant fight. It comes in waves, and I don't always know it's going on, which is really frustrating. I've gotten better at recognizing it. The ADHD problems and my depression go hand in hand.
>
> Depression is something you can't really see. It's a problem, and it's a serious thing. But since I don't have a really obvious medical condition, people don't take it seriously. It's still a medical problem. If I were to say (to a professor), 'I'm currently vomiting my brains out and I can't come to class,' they're going to be like, 'Okay fine, I guess. It's not great, but okay.' But if I say, 'My depression's acting up today; I can't go to class or I lost the fight with my ADHD brain today, and I kind of just don't want to do anything,' there's not much sympathy.

In addition to Jeremy's interior life with depression, he was also aware of the impression he made on other people. Jeremy reported:

> I feel like my depression, my bipolar, my Tourette's are seen in a room before I am. I always joke that I should make a little sign so people just understand or at least know. But you know sometimes it feels like people see

something, and they're looking at me going, 'What's wrong with that guy?'

Learning

The volunteers talked about their learning as internal and external access to the college curriculum. Their interior experiences interfered and interrupted the learning process. Externally, access to a college education involved peers, professors, and appropriate accommodations.

Nina recounted:

> Always I am having anxiety. It stops me from learning, and holds me back from going back to school. I feel like I am less than other people, and everybody looks at me. Even if I get A's, I don't feel it. I feel all the time that something is missing. Even the people who say I'm smart. Never tell anyone 'you're smart' because that makes it more miserable. Okay, I'm smart, so what. I don't know how to use it!

James shared some of his insights about maturing as a learner:

> I am learning what particularly I struggle with. I realize sometimes I make problems much bigger than they are, or I put obstacles in my way to prove to myself or to others that it's that difficult. I'll set myself up for failure

on purpose. But I can't keep feeling sorry for myself and making my own problems. It's just not helping me.

Emma was involved in an intense process of learning about herself, but that process was making it challenging to engage in her academic program. "I've finally started dealing with everything. I have so much I'm learning, which is why I think it's been so hard here at college." Susan spoke for all the participants when she said, "I've always been an eager to learn person. I couldn't stop learning. I didn't want to stop learning."

Progress

The participants discussed their progress with self-acceptance in the context of a college environment. Brittany received her initial diagnosis when she experienced a crisis in college:

> When I got to college, I had trouble, and I got diagnosed. I realized, 'Okay, I can't do what everyone else is doing.' And even though I want to do what everyone else is doing, I physically can't do it. I really want to succeed, but I know I can't succeed going down the same path as everyone else. And it's embarrassing. I'm going to be frank and say it's extremely embarrassing.

Emma was also diagnosed with a mental health disorder while attending her first college:

I knew something was wrong for a long time. I was still on the track to work doing something in the Middle East. I was so afraid I would lose my job opportunities. I also didn't want to admit that there was a problem. I finally admitted that it was okay and finally started talking about it, but I still didn't want the label. When I finally was okay with that and finally rationalized that, I started dealing with it.

When James started to take control of his learning, he found academics to be more meaningful.

College is just another progression, another chapter in a book. It comes with new sets of problems. I'm starting to realize what I need to do; prioritize my responsibilities and my commitments. I'm starting to set more goals, so it's easier to start seeing the light at the end of the tunnel, what I'm reaching for. It's not all just meaningless events that accumulate to nothing. There's actually something that's going to be gained at the end.

Change

The participants talked about change in terms of the lifetime interior changes that occurred with having mental health challenges, changes that took place in their lives, and their desire for change in attitudes toward mental illness. Brittany's symptoms were never fully managed. She disclosed, "I never know how I'm going to feel each day. I can't predict how I'm going to feel each hour or even every second! Things change really quickly." James stated that changes during his life contributed to an appreciation for his current circumstances:

> Doing good work feels good. I wouldn't want to have this change any other way. Even though my childhood was awful and I wouldn't want it for anyone else, I'm not spiteful about it. I'm not wishing it would have changed, because it gives me a better understanding and comprehension of what I need to do in order to succeed. It gives things more value, more merit.

Susan was adamant about attitude change on college campuses regarding mental illness, "It's not comfortable for people to talk about, but people need to get comfortable with being uncomfortable for anything to change!"

After the study participants so generously shared their experiences and their perspectives on those experiences, they concluded the study by providing recommendations for authentic ways to support students with comorbid attention deficits and psychiatric disorders in a college community.

Participant Recommendations for Support Practices

The participants initiated this study in part because they wanted people in the academic community to understand them better. They wanted their experiences and needs to be believed, and they wanted to educate others so that they in turn could have better access to an education. There was consensus among the volunteers that the entrée to educating college faculty and staff was to start a conversation. They found it valuable to take time on an individual basis to initiate discussions about the ways in which they learned, obstacles to learning, and ways to support their academic success. As Emma said, "I don't have all the answers, but we could all work together to come up with the answers." Because having these conversations every semester with every professor was often exhausting and stressful, the participants strongly recommended formally educating the general college community through regular trainings and workshops. It was hoped that with an educated campus, students with psychiatric disorders would become an ordinary, expected part of the community thus reducing the stigma and social risks of disclosing a mental illness.

Because mental illnesses were invisible medical disorders, the study participants proposed access to medical accommodations such as flexibility regarding academic requirements, which were available to students who experienced injury or physical illness. When students had episodes of active symptoms of a mental illness, the need for medical accommodations was real. In addition, the participants promoted alternative ways to demonstrate course mastery when needed. For example, if at some point during a semester managing symptoms became difficult, submitting a project or video instead of a paper could meet a course requirement. Occasionally a participant required hospitalization during a semester when a mental health problem needed comprehensive treatment. During such times, it was common practice to withdraw from classes. The need for hospitalizations interrupted academic progress and course withdrawals were recorded on official transcripts. Participants preferred offering incomplete grades with the option to continue with course work while in hospital. The incomplete grades would be replaced with a course grade upon completion. With remote learning, participants felt that this was a reasonable opportunity.

Understanding that college campuses were not therapeutic environments, the participants proposed addressing mental health on college campuses through facilitated support groups. The rationale was that these groups could relieve the sense of isolation that students with ADHD and coexisting psychiatric disorders frequently experience in the college environment. Study volunteers also noted that psychiatric emergencies often occur after business hours. For students who lived in campus residence halls, the only available responders to such emergencies were campus security officers. These officers may or may not have had adequate training to assist a student having a mental health crisis. The participants recommended that mental health counselors be assigned to after business hours to triage psychiatric emergencies.

It was interesting to note that the study participants made only a small number of recommendations. Cognizant that change was difficult, the participants were strategic in determining which practices potentially could best support their academic efforts. They asserted that these few changes would make significant differences in the quality of life during their academic lives.

Summary

A formal qualitative study was initiated by a group of adult college students who lived with attention deficit disorders and comorbid psychiatric disorders. These students were frequently frustrated in their attempts to make progress towards completing their college degrees. In addition to individual struggles with managing mental health challenges, their interactions with the college community also presented obstacles. With some urgency, these students agreed that they wanted members of the college community to get to know them. Increased understanding, they hoped, would reduce the stigma of mental illness on college campuses and support meaningful academic accommodations and practices to address their complex learning needs. Generously and courageously, seven students volunteered to be interviewed for the study. In their interviews, they shared intimate experiences of their internal lives with ADHD and mental illnesses. The study participants detailed their experiences with the academic community and the difficulties they faced when trying to assert their learning requirements. After facilitating a better understanding of people with mental illnesses through their narratives, these adults offered specific recommendations that would better support their academic progress. Above all, the study volunteers stressed taking time to get to know them.

COLLEGE SUPPORT
FACULTY PERSPECTIVES

CHAPTER 5

THE DANCE: TEACHER/LEARNER LEAD AND FOLLOW

Introduction

LIKE ELEMENTS OF dance, such as space, time, and energy, adult learners with ADHD and co-occurring mental health challenges need space to learn, time to learn, and energy to learn. Within a college academic support program developed specifically to address the needs of adult learners with complex challenges, these adult students engage with their support faculty in a dance to transform. Seven college faculty members, each having at least 20 years of teaching experience with adult learners and who provided academic support to adult students enrolled in the support program, participated in qualitative interviews to share their teaching practice.

Within the safety of the relationship, adult college students with ADHD and the professors who support them have the opportunity to challenge assumptions regarding disability, to make mistakes, and to connect to an openness to learning, which can create a space to learn with courage. As special educators, we are culturalized to determine students' needs; however, the joy of learning and teaching is to discover with our students their own courage to commit to who they really are as learners rather than who they think they should be (Brown, 2010). In our teaching practice, we strive to engage and support students in the paradox and ambiguity of being intellectually bright and having learning challenges. The professors interviewed for this chapter offer students the freedom to explore ambiguity and paradox and to be themselves. This exploration involves the whole person and active learning connects student and teacher to vulnerability, courage, compassion, and creativity. As teachers, it is our job to do the seeing with our students. Through radical presence, we are completely engaged in our students' processes for learning; pulling teaching and learning from their process. We tell students what we see as their stories unfold, supporting them in their efforts to learn about themselves, and we in turn are enriched by their stories.

Dialogue is integral to our practice when working with adult students with attention deficits. Through dialogue, these students develop habits of mind, which enable them to cope with their academic experiences and relinquish habits that create barriers to learning. Dialogue offers the teacher access to student meaning-making and creates a space where we as teachers can join our students in exploring assumptions about who they are as learners; in trying new learning approaches; and in acknowledging evidence of deep change. In this space students share their shame in having disabilities, their vulnerabilities when interacting with others, and their challenges when confronting academics. Most importantly, students disclose different ways they meet challenge, and this is where we as teachers discover their strengths.

Space

Adult college students with ADHD and coexisting psychiatric disabilities and the faculty who supported them created the space in which to learn. This space was student-centered, nonjudgmental, and accepting. Learners and teachers identified learning barriers and with authentic support worked together toward personal and academic growth.

Student-centered

As practitioners, it was important to help students make connections in the learning space and to be keen observers of that process. We left our egos outside the learning space, understanding that we did not control everything. Learning and teaching took on a life of its own, and the students often led in the dance. Chris encouraged her students to take the lead in determining goals for themselves:

> To sit down and talk to the students about what those goals might be and what interests them is very impor-

tant, and this is ongoing. The goals are not from the family, not from me, and not from another professor. They are student-generated. They have to be. It makes it important to them.

We were witnesses in the learning space. According to Grace:

> The hardest thing is allowing yourself not to jump in and fix things. You have to say, 'No, that's not my job right now. My job is to really look at this student.'
>
> You have to look for that light, that twinkle in their eye when they say something. Then you have to look beyond the words. 'Yeah, I danced the other day,' and you see that twinkle in their eye. You think, 'Dancing. This student loves to dance. Okay, how can we use dancing in writing?' You transfer that to other things when you see that light.

Judgement

A judgement-free space was essential to enabling students learning to learn. A non-judgmental environment was important in the teacher-student relationship as well as in teacher-to-teacher collaborations, which also benefitted students. Sam emphasized the role judgement played in her students' lives:

Judgement is huge. That's very important because for whatever reason they've been judged before and found lacking. Even for someone with parents with the best of hearts, the parents had become judgmental or they represented that judgmental mindset. 'Mom and Dad wanted me to go to college, and I didn't. I didn't make it.'

Leah elaborated on this notion that students have internalized the judgement of "found lacking":

I think this population especially is filled with such shame about the fact that they still haven't finished their degrees. They have this sort of embarrassment of failure. Cutting through all that just to have them work on the academics is often a challenge because part of them wants to do it and be successful, and then part of them is judging themselves. My big thing is I always try to establish a sense of safety and that I'm not judging.

Deborah made the point that when working with adult students with ADHD, it was important to provide judgement-free space for fellow colleagues doing similar work:

We shared both our successes and our failures. We could really and truly question our own assumptions and talk with each other without fear of being judged. It wasn't like we had to pretend we knew everything. We didn't.

Acceptance

In a judgement-free space, acceptance of the teacher for their students and acceptance of students for themselves was critical to gaining access to learning. Leah described helping students work through shame by "helping them to accept where they are and that they have different ways of getting where they need to be." Providing a framework for acceptance, Deborah referred to Carl Rogers' concept of unconditional positive regard. "I think they were all craving that," asserted Deborah. "It's a combination of loving concern for them and acceptance; the presumption that they are good, worthy human beings." Illustrating unconditional positive regard, Deborah related the following story:

> One of my students had a very hard time. She'd had an abusive childhood. She had spent time on the streets. So, she had very much struggled. One day she decided to bring me poetry that she had written. There was some beautiful poetry in there, and some of it was painful poetry about her childhood abuse. I cried. I remember later on she said to me, 'The thing that you gave me most was when you cried about my poetry.' So, it's a simple thing like that. I didn't plan it. I didn't want to cry, really, with my student, but her poetry made me cry. I think what she meant was there was genuine feeling for what she had gone through and genuine concern. She became very successful. She became a lawyer.

Distilling a complex process, Anne simply stated, "You accept who that person is and their experiences, and they have to accept what they need to continue in life."

Psychological Barriers

As discussed in earlier chapters, coexisting mental health challenges presented barriers to student progress in the learning space. The teachers interviewed were cognizant of these barriers and provided safe spaces where students were able to examine these difficulties in the context of academics.

Leah pointed out, "When the emotional stuff gets in the way, you can't have access to the academic stuff." She related a story about one of her students who was a brilliant writer, but was "so tortured":

> School was such a psychological battle. He had the academic skills, but he'd failed so many times. It was all his psychological barriers. So, sometimes even if the skills are there, it doesn't matter when they have those barriers.

Chris added:

> You know the students with emotional issues have the aptitude to do the work, but they can't get past whatever else is going on in their lives to get to the content area. Very frustrating. I find that most of these students are very intelligent and very capable, but they're in bed all

day because they can't get up. That's terribly challenging. Getting back into the game after struggling with emotional issues, I value that. I value the fact that they can come out of the hole that they might put themselves in or fall in because it's hard to climb out. It's like a big monster is pulling your foot back down.

For adult students with coexisting psychiatric disorders, Deborah stated that the societal stigma of having these challenges created, initially, an additional barrier for some of her students to disclose their struggles. According to Deborah:

Often times even though they know they have coexisting disorders, they don't tell me about them upfront. They just come in and say, 'Oh, I have ADHD.' The ADHD is not the only reason they didn't write that paper. It may have been that they were paralyzed with anxiety or depression. As time goes on and they learn to trust, then they can tell you other symptoms that they're experiencing.

Creating emotionally safe spaces in which to build trusting relationships enabled adult students to deal with psychological barriers. As Chris said, "Sometimes it takes a while for that trust to build, but I think for the most part it comes after a while." Anne added, "You establish that comfort level, because students have to be comfortable before they open up. They're not going to open up if they're not comfortable." In working with her adult students, Deborah asserted:

> I think that for a lot of our adults, it was the first time they had had, in an academic setting, safety. They had always felt threatened, afraid, scared they were going to get called on, afraid to turn in a paper. Some of them would write papers and wouldn't turn them in because they were afraid of the reaction or ashamed of what they wrote. Many of my students had been treated as if they were lesser students and incapable of any kind of advanced intellectual work. It was not true, but they felt that way about themselves for many years because they were treated that way. They were humiliated in school.

Despite psychological barriers, Sam spoke about the fundamental optimism of her adult students:

> They had hope. They still had hope because they came back (to school). I think if they didn't have hope, they couldn't make it. It's also a matter of my showing there is hope, too.

Authentic Student Support

In the space of authentic support for adult students with ADHD, the first task was often to determine where each student was situated in life and the external stressors that might affect their academic progress. Anne's initial conversations included the following:

If they're older adults and they're married, then you need to talk about the support they're getting from their partners. Do they have children? The financial part of it when they're adults is another issue. How are they going to manage their house, their family, going to school? Are they working?

Additional services were also identified to support students beyond the work that took place in the learning space. As trust developed, faculty study participants frequently encouraged their students to access mental health counselors when they were not in therapy. Deborah stated, "If they don't have counseling already, sometimes you can gently suggest it, and sometimes they'll choose to do that." Sam would tell her students:

We all have baggage. We all have baggage somewhere. So, we just work on it. If they're not going to a therapist, they usually have had a history so I try to encourage them to get that going again.

In addition to guiding her students to connect with a therapist, Chris also worked with students to:

Direct them to the right place, to the right person, in the right direction. Moving them to get them out of whatever it is that's in their way, moving forward, dealing with that brick wall with continued support, leading them to the right people to do the right things.

This meant augmenting her support by helping students contact subject specific tutors, organizations that expanded interests and social networks, or services that facilitated internships and career exploration.

Once the students' initial needs were determined, a dynamic, collaborative process developed between the study participants and their students, where students and teachers learned from each other—the hallmark of authentic support. Deborah said that sometimes she, "Just listened to them and had a conversation about their week. We'd talk about what they experienced and their feelings about it." Through conversation, Deborah discovered with her students the learning mechanisms and teaching approaches that suited each individual student:

> It's organic. The how-to is in there, but that's not the key to unlocking the learning. It's not the key to the success. It's the "why" and the "why not," getting at that, as well as, identifying the things that can block.

Leah added:

> The process is the task of identifying what they can do well. Do they have any confidence anywhere in any part of their life? My big thing is I always try to establish this sense of safety; that I'm not judging; I have compassion for their situation, and I understand the situation that they're in. I'm there to support them. I think for me that's a big part of my process, and then, really, it's whatever unfolds.

The work of learning and teaching was not simply applying strategies and techniques. To address the complexities of adult students with multiple needs, a deeper dive was required to examine students' learning in order to provide authentic support. Deborah went on to assert:

> What doesn't work is forcing, predetermining outcomes, and criticizing. They are so tender and so vulnerable to criticism. And they cover it up. They're masters at covering up vulnerabilities. Gently help them come to awareness of something that's in their way, some behavior or whatever it is that's getting in their way, without criticizing it. I just found that criticizing never worked.

Deborah and Grace both emphasized the importance of emphasizing the positive while acknowledging limitations within the relationships with their students so that they did not over help their students or attempt to rescue them. Grace gave the example:

> I had a student who would put his head down every time he came into my office. I always said, 'Pick your head up. You're worth picking your head up.' Those kinds of things are important, but always putting it in a positive way, even if you're kind of saying, 'That doesn't go in this class.' And he didn't react to it, as it was. That's was not easy for me, because I did want to jump in and make it better. It was not easy for me at

all, but that's what I learned as a teacher: to be able to do that without jumping in and fixing.

It was difficult to witness a student's suffering. Grace's response was to sit with that student in support and facilitate an experience where the student was indeed able to manage. Chris spoke to the foundation of authentic support:

> I, hopefully, provide an environment where they trust me. They can tell me what's really going on and know that I'm here to help them. I'm not here to get mad at them or reprimand them. I'm only here to help and support them to get through whatever obstacles they encounter and get to that content area, which sometimes seems minimal with what they have going on.

Collegial Support

In addition to providing a supportive learning space for adult students with coexisting ADHD and psychiatric disorders, the participants in this study described a space where they authentically supported each other in their teaching practice with this population. Anne said it was important to "know enough to get whatever support you needed." In other words, as a professional, it was prudent to seek help when encountering problems. Anne continued:

> Hopefully you're in a place, and you should be, where you're able to talk to other people about where you're

coming from or if you have a question. That's really important. I did that. When I was questioning something, I could always go to a colleague and say, 'Look I want you to look at this and double-check me.' I mean, be open enough about yourself so you can have somebody look at your work and say, 'You know, I think you should look at this and see where it goes.' I think that's important too. Besides, you need the emotional support.

Grace and Deborah emphasized the value of peer support. True support expanded and enriched their teaching practice and minimized the sense of isolation while doing difficult work. Deborah declared:

I had fabulous colleagues. We shared both our successes and our failures. We could really and truly question our own assumptions. We could really talk with each other without fear of being judged. So, it wasn't like we had to pretend we knew everything; we didn't. We could say to each other, 'I'm not succeeding with this student. I don't know what to do.' We could work things out together, and talk to somebody who would say, 'But…' and help you see the other side. I think that authentic support was one of the things that allowed us to do this work in the way we did. It's deep work. You can't do this as a lone ranger.

Grace added, "We had really great conversations about the work. We had fascinating conversations! I think that was really powerful." She continued:

> I couldn't have done the deep work being isolated. I couldn't have done it, and there's no reason to do it that way. You have to build relationships; people have to help you build them. To me, that was what kept me going. Having teachers where you weren't afraid to say, 'I f…ed up,' and they wouldn't judge you. When I felt like, 'Oh god, I'm exhausted,' or I needed to cry,' or… You know what I mean? Not being afraid to cry, and saying, 'You know, I had a student that touched those buttons in me.' And I could go on. It was peer work. I feel really lucky that I had that. I needed that kind of support, and I got it.

Time

Frank points out that time management is a simplistic way to consider time when working with adult students with ADHD. Progress towards academic outcomes is never a straight, steady trajectory. Bodensteiner (2019) states that one of the elements of dance, time, involves relationship or connection to music, movement through time, rhythm, and tempo. In the learning/teaching environment of adult students with ADHD, the student and teacher move through time together in the learning process. They develop a relationship or connection to each other and invest in the process. Teacher and student determine the tempo or pace of learning through identifying teachable moments as they move toward student-centered goals. A rhythm of questioning, then sitting and being present with the student to reflect on learning is critical to transformative work.

Connection

The study participants subscribed to the tenet that developing relationships with their students was essential to their work. If they did not build strong connections, students would not attempt the strategies offered or take learning risks. Anne described this foundational work:

It doesn't happen immediately. You get to know them; you get to know their wishes; you get to know what they're like; and you make them feel comfortable enough to be open with you. You try to establish the relationship. You know when you're connecting, and so you know you're going to go someplace with the student.

Sam stated, "If I don't have a relationship, I'm not as successful." Her relationships with her students provided security and confidence from which to extend their connections to others. Seemingly small obstacles like contacting the college registrar were overwhelming to some of Sam's students. Facilitating and supporting smaller connections enabled them to build competences in order to persist. Sam described a situation where one of her students needed to contact the registrar:

> There was the issue of a grade not being changed, and I said, 'Well, have you done it?' 'No, I haven't done it yet,'

replied the student. 'So, let's call over to the Registrar's office.' What I did was we called over, and of course no one was available. I left her name and number, and they said they would get back to her. So, that makes it a connection. She doesn't have to make that step. They'll step out to her.

Chris talked about the importance of connection not only between her and her students, but also connection among other adult students with ADHD. Facilitating that connection involved offering regularly scheduled group meetings where students came together to discuss issues of adult learners and develop relationships among group members:

> Connecting with the other students, I think, in group is so important. They look around campus, and it feels to them as if everybody else knows each other. Other students are already connected whereas they're not, which is how they perceive it. If they're in a group of all students who are older, they're all in the same boat, and they all have something in common already. It's nice that they can come together and get to know one another and connect that way. They really need to feel a connection, not just to us but to other students in other areas of campus. Very important. I think that group is key. I really do.

Chris provided the example of a group of women who stated that they felt isolated as students. Through participation in the group, they developed friendships. She said, "I was so thrilled to see those women rooming together. What a difference that made in their attitudes toward college, happily coming back the next semester and looking forward to it. Huge difference!"

Frank stayed connected to one of his students for many years, which enabled the student to create new connections:

> Adult students with ADHD need validation that what they are doing is legitimate and important. For Stuart, simply staying connected in academic circles is important, whether in graduate classes or staying in one course. Being part of a community is significant.

Grace's Buddhist practice guided her teaching with adult students with ADHD and her questions were foundational to the work:

> I think some parts of my Buddhist practice are important like connection, compassion, and presence. It is so important to be present. I think they go side-by-side. I had these students, and we took the same path together. Where do they make the connections? What do those connections look like? What is our connection?

Goals

Goal setting was a mechanism to move adult students with ADHD through the time of their academic programs; however, goals originated with the student. Throughout the learning experience, both short-term and long-term goals were dynamic so as to accommodate and adjust to increased student self-awareness, emerging learning strengths, and evolving learning needs. Anne began at the beginning when meeting her students, saying, "First thing I do is ask them, 'What is your goal? Where do you want to be? What do you want to do?' Then I feed in what I think, but it always starts with them."

Deborah articulated the process of goal setting as an ongoing:

> Dynamic process that has to be constantly moving, responding, and adjusting but with a core of stability. It's an interesting mixture when you think of it. So, at the beginning of the semester, I asked my new students what their goals were; what did they want to achieve? Some of them really didn't even know how to do that. They didn't know what they wanted because nobody had even asked them that question. But those goals they identified on that first day might change radically. So, the first day a student might say, 'I want to learn to write papers better.' Okay, I can do that with you. But as time went on, the goals would be to help them to come to, 'Yeah, one of my goals that I would like to see is I would like to become a more confident writer. I would like to trust my own ideas more. I would like to believe that I can write.' Those were the goals that I think we really spent a lot of time working on. We kept adjusting them, keeping in mind the interplay with their actual course demands. Students don't develop

self-confidence because somebody tells them they're great. They develop it because they achieved something and that feeling of competence feeds itself. We always looked at all their syllabi together and talked about which things they felt independent in and which things were going to need my support. The goals are a combination of personal goals for each student, of academic goals imposed from the outside by the teacher, by the professors in the classroom, and then of the changing goals as the time went on, as the days went on. Sometimes, for some students who are suffering from depression, the goal might just be getting up in the morning and coming to class.

Chris also identified goals with her students through conversation:

I actually have them write them down at the beginning of each semester as part of their educational plan. Goal setting is important. They need to know why they're doing what they're doing and the little steps to take along the way to reach their goals. The students who do best have goals in mind. To sit down and talk to them about what those goals might be and what interests them is very important and that's ongoing. The goals are not from the parents; they're not from me; they're not from another professor. They are student-generated. They have to be. It makes the goals important to them.

PERSPECTIVES ON ACADEMIC SUPPORT

Chris continued:

> I let the students take the lead. They're all different. Can I sit down and talk to someone about their coursework right away? Maybe, maybe not. Maybe there are other things we need to discuss first. How they got here; why they're here; what was their journey; where are they going—if they know? That's an ongoing process; it's all ongoing. A lot of conversation, a lot of goal-setting, both small and short-term and long-term. Constantly revisiting. What do they want to do? It could be moving into a new major or just getting their coursework done consistently. Reaching out to professors, if that's something they struggle with. The short-term goals are just as important as their long-term. Those little successes along the way add up. How to keep them moving towards success and moving toward their goal, rather than stopping or going backward.

For Sam's students, discussing goals was a way to learn intentional thinking:

> The reason we start to talk about goals is to get them thinking about goals and not because they have to follow them. I say to them, 'I want you to give me two academic goals you'd like and one personal goal you'd like to accomplish.' Usually, they'll easily come up with the personal one like, 'I'm going to go to the gym.' Then I'll say, 'Well, that doesn't tell me how many times a week you're going. Let's be more specific.' So, we start

with those goals, but in the end, I don't really follow them. I follow where they are day-by-day, and pick them up where they are, the goal they accomplished that day. We're setting up goals, and we're going to have a direction. That's how I use them.

Frank also helped students learn strategic thinking through goal setting:

My process is student-driven based on his or her goals whether employment related or academic in nature. I discuss goals early on with students, and often they are woven into a contract. I also have students identify and write down goals they wish to set and achieve, and they are referred to throughout our semester. I recall working with a student where the goal for the student was a passing grade on a CPA exam. In that case, my goal was also that he pass or better his score—but also, a number of test-taking strategies were more explicit in the goals based on the examination and his previous practice test scores.

In Leah's experience, goals were established by her adult students based on a sense of urgency. Leah explained, "They need to acquire a certain skill, or they need to complete a certain task, or they need to do this class." She gave the example of a student who had completed all her coursework for graduation except for passing Statistics. Leah recalled:

I think she took statistics four times. She could do everything else, but the thing she needed was this barrier. How was she going to figure it out? She tried it at a different college; she tried it with a different professor. This was the task she needed to accomplish.

Leah added that goals were not just for students. She said, "To have compassion, instill some confidence, and help students understand their capabilities are always my huge, ongoing goals as a teacher with these students." Helping students understand their capabilities enabled students to learn about themselves in deeper ways. Grace contributed her perspective regarding goal setting:

> When I first get an adult student, they give the goals they think they should have.
>
> I think goals are good, but I think paying attention to our deepest selves is the most important goal. Some goals make sense, but most of them are more 'shoulds' than 'who I am in this world, and what I really want.' I'm not against goals, but I think you have to be careful they don't freeze you into what you think you want to be, rather than what you are.

For the participants in this study and their adult students, establishing goals and objectives and working towards particular outcomes were never linear processes. As Deborah stated:

Sometimes what was needed was stretching yourself, too. These students stretched me. It didn't just go one way. I had to learn that there's more than one nice linear way to do things, and they would still come up with a good product. Certainly, I had to keep finding ways to give them guidance so their ADHD wouldn't rule them.

Grace continued:

I didn't express the learning outcomes; they expressed it. Some of them, even the ones who weren't writers, wrote the most beautiful things about what they learned about themselves. They always surprised me, because I wasn't even sure that was happening. So, they know what outcomes are real and not real.

Chris's students were frequently nonlinear thinkers. She said it best regarding goals and goal achievement, "You need to wait and see where they're going, and go with them."

Investment

Investment in adult students with ADHD took time. Because the professors who participated in this study saw the potential in these students and believed in their abilities to realize their potential, they invested in a process that supported discovery of abilities, which for some, was transformational. Deborah described the challenging path she embarked on with her students as they explored their talents, as well as, their obstacles. At times, she believed in the student:

> . . . more than himself or herself. I saw this tremendous potential. Sometimes I struggled to find the way to help them unlock it, or find some way to be able to discard the modes of thinking that were holding them back. The painful emotions that were holding them back. Once they started to believe in themselves, they believed they could do it. They wanted to write that paper well.

"Believing in their capability to change," enabled Sam to persist with her students:

> I think you have to be dedicated. Because I think that there are going to be slip-ups, and you have to be willing to reach out and pull them back in, and say, 'Oops, that didn't work for you. Let's try something else.'

Leah acknowledged that her adult students with learning challenges and emotional complexities, who found college work daunting, having someone who was invested in them was critical to their investment in themselves as learners:

> These students, I just feel so much more invested in their success because for them college work is defining. I think, 'Yeah, I'd want somebody to help me in this

way.' It's not a lot of sweat off my back, and I know this concentrated intention and attention to them can make a huge difference. I just feel like yeah, why wouldn't I do that for someone?

I enjoy the students' commitment; their seriousness and dedication; the stamina that it takes for them to be in this situation and still be trying. Look at Edward! He's always trying to figure something out, fit something in, and try something new, and it's exhausting! So, these students are on a level of dedication where I just have such admiration for them.

Grace described the initial investment in her students as "messy." She asserted, "I don't try to clean it up before I really engage with the mess." In order for learning to emerge, take form, take shape, and find direction, engaging the mess took time and courage. Students demonstrated courage as they allowed someone to witness their vulnerability and persist with sorting out the mess. Sometimes part of Frank's investment was encouraging his students to invest themselves in the process of exploring and identifying learning strengths and difficulties. According to Frank, "Hard work and determination needed to be cornerstones." When his students revealed what they loved, this became the starting point of their investment, and then they were able to dedicate themselves to the hard work needed to realize their ambitions. Frank told the story of a young woman who became deeply invested in her own learning and growth in part because of the relationship he had established with her, "Erin very much needed an opportunity to speak with someone about ADHD and her academic history, a history that did in no way accurately reflect her incredible aptitudes. In conversations with her, she saw professional validation of her strengths."

Knowing

All of the study participants endorsed knowing each of their students wholistically as fundamental to the students' progress in the college environment. Taking time to understand their students in deep ways supported students' understanding of themselves, which led to enhanced, sustained learning. Anne elaborated on her process of getting to know her students:

> The first thing is you just talk to them. Get to know what they think of themselves.
>
> When you're only looking at that student as having ADHD or a learning difficulty, whatever you want to call it, you're making a big mistake because it's how they deal with life. You need to get to know their experience and the student as a whole. What are they dealing with and how are they dealing with everything? It relates to their learning processing; how they process information. So, you have to go beyond the classroom and look at all their experiences.

> You just get to know them and then you go from there. Usually, going from there is where they're going to take you. They're going to take you; you're not going to take them. You can influence them and you can put up directions or guidelines, or even fences so they won't go off the road, but they're going to guide you. And you better be ready to go for it.

Chris cautioned that knowing her students influenced the ways in which she spoke to each of them:

> You have to be careful what you say to each student. It's knowing the students well enough to know how to move them forward, really listening to them and getting to know them well enough to be able to help them the best way possible. You have to approach them all differently based on where they're coming from and how they perceive things.

For all the participants, knowing their students enabled them to do the analysis of their students' needs often in the moment, and deploy flexible thinking and problem-solving to meet those needs.

Pausing

Sometimes it was important to take stock of students' circumstances, to sit with students and acknowledge where they were situated. The pause before proceeding with academic demands often informed the means to proceed. Deborah provided an example:

> ADHD was not the only reason they didn't write that paper. It may have been that they were just paralyzed with anxiety or depression. It was important to pick up the clues on that and then know the right questions to ask, so they can get in touch with that. Sometimes, like we all do, you don't even know how you're feeling until somebody sits you down and takes a little quiet time to say, 'How are you feeling? Let's talk about why you haven't started the paper. What do you think? Why do you think you haven't started it?' They might start off with something superficial like, 'I've just been too busy.' You find ways to keep asking the question until finally they admit that they're afraid to do it, or their anxiety is too strong.

Chris found it critical:

> ... to just sit back and listen. You need to sit back and allow them to talk, but stay focused yourself. Can I sit down and talk to someone about their coursework right away? Maybe, maybe not. Maybe there are other things we need to discuss first. The beauty of this work is they can sit, think about what they need to say and do, talk about it, get advice, and mull things over for a while if they need to.

Pausing was often essential to making academic progress.

Tempo

The tempo or speed of learning was not a linear process to academic outcomes. Bumps along the way had to be identified and dealt with, and individual learning differences had to be accommodated. It was important to acknowledge the individual growth of a student especially when the tempo of their experience did not fit their assumptions about academic elements that defined success. Sam told this story:

> I had a student come in and she said, 'This has been a complete wash, this year!' I said, 'Oh, no! You have achieved marvelous change. You spent a lot of time working on your individual growth, and your academic growth got halted a little. But you didn't completely give up on your academics. You just didn't do as well as you thought you were going to do. But you had growth in your career, and you had growth in your understanding of your relationship with your parents.' So, I listed all the things, and she went away thinking 'Well, I wasn't a total failure.' And then I also had to explain to her that college isn't just about academics. So, I think she went out with a positive, but I don't know how long she held it. That's my other concern.

When Anne encountered obstacles that interrupted a student's progress, she, respectfully, took a firmer hand in guiding her student through the challenge:

> I've been proven wrong a few times, but I often know when to go where the student's going and when to

direct the student, or do both at the same time. When I recognize a problem, I discuss it at the appropriate time. If the issue is getting in the way of their work, I may make suggestions more strongly than I would other times and then I give them time to consider our conversation.

Chris and Deborah asserted that adult students needed time to strategize and really examine the path they were taking with someone who supported them. Regarding college enrollment, Chris stated, "I see more and more students who take a longer amount of time to get through or start to attend later in life." When adult students were enrolled, Deborah described the tempo of the work:

> I had a responsibility to help students succeed in college, but I never decided ahead of time or predetermined what the outcome would be. You listen. You talk. You explore. You change as you go along, determined by the student. The student leads. Sometimes you try to bend the path a little bit in a certain direction. If they're open to it, great. If they're not, you're just wasting your time.

Energy

In dance, movement through space and time requires energy, the third element. Energy of dance involves flow of movement, quality of movement, weight of movement, and force of action or attack. Like dance, where learning takes place (space) and when learning occurs (time) also necessitate how learning is accomplished (energy) (Bodensteiner, 2019). Faculty engage adult students with complex ADHD in a kindness-based, transformative curriculum that can be compared to these aspects of energy in dance.

Compassion

The flow or give and take of energy in the participants' teaching practice involved compassion. They emphasized the fundamental need for compassion in building relationships with their students, the foundation of the learning process. "Compassion and empathy are key!" according to Frank. Students often entered the learning process shouldering painful histories, and it was essential that their teachers understood their burdens. Leah described compassion in her practice:

> Adults have so many unique situations. My big thing is I always try to establish a sense of safety and that I'm not judging. I have compassion for their situation; I understand the situation they're in; and I'm there to support them. That's a big part of my process. I hope through compassion to instill some confidence and help them understand their capabilities.

Grace summarized, "You practice love. And that's compassion."

Flexibility

The flow of energy in learning and teaching also required flexibility. Anne asserted, "As a teacher, you need to be very flexible in what you're doing, and flexibility is usually where the student is at." Sometimes a student's employment circumstances interrupted or slowed academic progress. Frank found he needed to take time with some of his students to examine the ways in which their learning challenges affected their experiences in a work environment and then relate these experiences to academics. Frank stated, "In working with adults, I am always cognizant that many places of employment have little knowledge or support for learning difficulties. We talk about 'real life' implications of such things." Such conversations helped students resume progress in school and provided support for improved job performance.

Because the context in which adult students learned frequently changed, professors in this study stated they had to be nimble to address changing needs. Leah defined flexibility in her work with students:

> Flexibility is the ability to keep reconsidering the context every time you go in to work with a student. You like to think that some of the strategies, these sort of practical things, can be universally transferred. If you're rigid you're going to be having a hard time. The context is changing, and the student's internal context is changing too. You have to consider the context of what you're doing. Maybe what you did last time is not going to work today. I think we all sometimes feel, 'I

just want to get that formula, do the recipe.' Everybody wants the latest thing that's going to work, and there's no latest thing. Even when you think you figured it out, you're going to go in the next day and that's not going to work. Context is constantly changing.

Leah then illustrated the necessity of flexibility when she helped her student prepare for a state licensing examination for social workers:

Flexibility was critical. I had to reframe a whole test situation for my student who had to pass the social work exam in order to keep her job. In that case literally, every week I was saying, 'What am I going to do next to help her? What's another way that I can help her manage this situation?' We would try everything externally that was possible: the reader, digital study materials, extended time, snacks, every possible external accommodation. I had to come up with strategies, not really to take the test, because I knew the concrete things to do in a test like that, but more psychological strategies so it was not such an overwhelming, life-or-death situation.

When the internal context changed, professors supporting adult students needed to be flexible, but also had to know ways to address internal challenges. Academic assistance took a different form when depression or anxiety was in charge. Deborah stated, "You do have to have theoretical knowledge to work properly and be able to assess

and switch pathways to reach them…The art of teaching."
A seemingly small accommodation could be enormously
supportive. Deborah provided an example:

> If somebody's missed a class and then you send them
> a stern email, 'You weren't here today! Blahblahblah-
> blahblah.' The next class that's scheduled, what do you
> think they're going to do? They're not going to come!
> We all avoid unpleasant confrontations. So, then you
> learn to say, 'Oh I missed you! Hope you're okay. If
> there's anything you need, please call me, and if you
> have a chance, let me know what happened.' Punitive
> doesn't work; criticism doesn't work; being didactic
> doesn't work. Inflexibility doesn't work.

Listening

Another aspect of dance was the quality of the energy
exerted. In learning and teaching, the quality of those experiences began with and depended on listening. The study
participants unpacked the listening process. First, Anne
stressed the importance of:

> Knowing your biases, because we all have them. Know
> enough to recognize them and put them in their proper
> place. You really have to have enough sense of self to be
> able to see that person. Look at the student. See what
> they're experiencing. Feel what they're experiencing.
> Respect what they're saying. Really listen to them. As

part of a caring practice, listening is fundamental to the work with adult students.

Deborah followed advice that David A. Kolb offered at a professional conference: ask, don't tell when working with adult students, "You may be hopeful that the student is going to come to a particular knowledge through asking, but you ask in a way that you're listening to them. 'What do you think of this?'"

Deborah also stated that she went home from work tired every day because she was listening so intently:

> Every minute I had to be fully present. I had to be thinking and changing in midstream. If you're really a good listener and you're really paying attention to what they're saying they want to do, you can figure out the way that the student is leading.

Chris was specific when describing the way she listened to her adult students with ADHD:

> I think it is important to just sit back and listen. Kind of allow them to talk in circles until they get to the point. It can be trying at times, but you need to let them do that because that's how they think. By the time they get to their point you say, 'Oh, okay. This was where you were going.' You need to sit back and allow them to do that, but stay focused yourself because you have to follow what they're saying. I respect that. They're not

linear thinkers for the most part. So, you need to wait and listen to where they're going. And go with them.

Like her colleagues, Grace listened in a deeper way:

I try to listen in a different kind of way, so I can reflect back to the student what I hear. I listen to their story, the backstory, and the story they're involved in now. I listen and reflect what I see. My job is to really look at the student; really listen to this student; and really see who they are. A student knows when you're there with them.

Love

The quality of energy in the learning/teaching relationship was fueled by love. All the subjects in this study loved their teaching practice with their adult students with ADHD. Chris loved watching her students "grow and mature; come into their own. I loved seeing the confidence build. Loved that!" Deborah loved working with adults "right from the beginning." She approached them with "nurturing love," a caring that encouraged students "to come back the next day and the next day and the next day."

Anne spoke for everyone when she shared:

There's a lot of satisfaction when a student finally gets it together; stands on their own two feet; and finds themselves. I think there's nothing more rewarding.

I love what I do. I mean I just love it! I honestly don't know how anybody can do it if you don't love it.

Patience

Weight as an aspect of energy in dance looked at heaviness and gravity or lightness and upward movement. Weight in the learning and teaching process was at times extremely heavy and at other times gratifyingly light when students moved upward in their progress. This weight was often shouldered in patience. The study participants identified patience as a critical component to their process with students. In addition to "humor, compassion, and empathy," Frank cited patience as key to forging relationships with his students, which also facilitated "keeping their goals not only in my mind, but in their minds as well." The participants framed patience in a particular way. Deborah stated that nurturing love allowed her to be patient with her students, but patience was:

> Not the kind where I'm sort of squirming inside, and I'm trying to be patient. It's the ability to let somebody be themselves, and wait it out. It's caring and openness, a willingness to really follow their lead.

Patience was not always employed in teaching academics. Chris stated that the teacher needed to be prepared for this:

Many times, it's not about academics. The academics are the easy part. If you're just doing the paper, if you're just getting through that chapter, that's the easy part. It's getting them to be able to work on those things that can be challenging.

Sam agreed:

I find that, especially with students with ADHD, they're bright, and so helping them in a content, tutoring way is not an effective way to help them because they feel insulted. So, I try to let them set the parameters of how we're going to work. I had one student who I wondered why he was in business, because he struggled and he had severe ADHD. After two years, he told me what his passion was and what he wanted. I said, 'Finally!' to myself. It does take time, and that's why I said patience was very important.

Leah identified patience as largely lacking in adult students' learning experiences.

My older students who've been literally and figuratively traumatized by their educational experiences have experienced no compassion and had no patience and no understanding. I acknowledge that from the start, 'Well it must have sucked for you.' Yet they come back to school. Despite all of it, they come back. I just think this whole idea about being patient and meeting them where they're at is critical.

Focus

A final aspect of energy in dance was attack, which meant that movement could be sudden or sustained. Learning could be sudden or sustained: a sudden burst of creativity, a moment of clarity, or sustained effort to achieve insight and understanding of self or an academic discipline. Difficulties with focus and sustained effort in school were hallmarks of learners with complex ADHD. The participants worked with their students to support or discover ways to focus so that they were able to sustain the energy needed to achieve satisfying results. Grace asserted, "By practicing focus, being open, and letting grace in the room," her students and she "had wonderful learning conversations every day."

Some of Chris's adult students were:

> . . . a little more focused. Goal-oriented. They know what they want to do in life, for the most part. They've had more experiences. I think if they're still in school and still seeking out a degree when they're 25, 30, 40, they really want it at that point. Some of them are still searching though. It's interesting to work with them, and if they don't have a focus, helping them to find it. I love it when they come to me on the first day not knowing what the heck they want to do, and by the time they finish they're focused. They have goals. They know what they want to do, whether it's grad school or a career choice.

Strengths

Maintaining focus to persist in school was more easily supported when student efforts were built on their strengths. As a means of attack in the learning process, all the study participants stressed the importance of identifying and building upon strengths. In Chris's view, student interests were indicators of student strengths. She helped her students articulate their interests, which informed their goals and provided direction for sustained effort. Leah acknowledged that this was quite difficult. "When students don't know what their strengths are; they don't think they're good at anything; you have to find somewhere to start and work from there." Understanding the challenges of identifying and realizing strengths, Grace introduced a writing exercise during initial student meetings when she "looked for the light that came in their eyes." Over time her process was:

> To get deeper and deeper with them. Have them really learn to see themselves, in some ways differently. And see their strengths, but as they're acting on them or talking about them.

As strengths were revealed, Deborah's students often surprised her:

> Some of my students would come up with these very creative views and products. During the course of our work, students would show abilities that sometimes hadn't ever been uncovered before or that they kept secret.

When students did not have a vision for themselves because they had yet to recognize their strengths, Sam started at the beginning:

> I become more developmental and look at, 'Okay, what's your passion? What do you like to do?' It's so hard to get them to admit to loving something. It's amazing. But over time they begin to say what they like and what they don't like.
>
> It is partially time, partially just being supportive, waiting, helping them find something, and talking about what excites them. I tell my students, 'If you're interested, you have a passion, you can learn!'

Considering the many aspects of energy employed by the study participants in order to work with adult students who have complex ADHD, Anne summarized it best:

> The best teachers I know are the ones who (when they have the background education) listen to their students; who are perceptive of their students; who know when to go where the student's going and when to direct the student (or do both at the same time); and who are willing to go to other people, other colleagues and ask question, double-check themselves if they feel the need.

Summary

Comparing academic support for adults with complex ADHD to elements of dance accounted for the space, time, and energy necessary for learning and teaching to occur between students and their support professors. Through qualitative research interviews, seven faculty who worked with adult college students in an academic support program, shared their teaching practice. A hallmark of their practice was reciprocity in their relationships with their students. They respectfully recognized and facilitated their students' needs to take the lead in their learning and then carefully assessed those moments when they took the lead in order to integrate various interventions. Leading and following in learning and teaching was only successful when both partners developed a strong relationship based on trust and the teachers' deep understanding of their students.

Professors created a space to learn that was student-centered and judgement free. A safe space enabled students with their teachers to explore and address the many challenges and barriers that accompanied living with ADHD. These explorations and subsequent learning required time; time to build the student/professor relationship, time to invest in the learning process, and time to manage anticipated and unexpected obstacles to progress. Sometimes students needed to pause and reflect on their learning. At other times students made steady, outward progress towards their goals. Energy essential for learning and teaching involved the flow of give and take between teachers and their students, which was based on compassion, and flexibility in accommodating changing contexts of students' internal and external lives. Deep listening and love of the student and the work were foundational to the energy to learn. For students and professors, exercising patience with themselves and each other provided the stamina for sustained effort. Students realizing and using their strengths powered their achievements and established new identities of competent, accomplished students.

CHAPTER 6

TRANSFORMATION: REWRITING THE INTERNAL SCRIPT

IN THE PREVIOUS chapter, the teaching-learning experience between adult students with complex ADHD and their support teachers was compared to the elements of dance where space, time, and energy were integrated, thus creating interdependent environments that facilitated transformational learning. Mezirow and Taylor (2009) defined *transformative learning* as learning that "transformed problematic frames of reference to make them more inclusive, discriminating, reflective, open, and emotionally able to change" (p. 22). Transformative learning was the adult learning and teaching model that the study participants in the previous chapter followed. It lent itself naturally to their teaching practice. The relationship between teacher and student was fundamental to the process and provided the foundation for examining assumptions, explaining frames of reference, and developing new habits of mind (Mezirow & Taylor, 2009). Through learning conversations, students and professors established new truths regarding individual competencies. "Dialogue becomes the medium for critical reflection to be put into action, where experience is reflected on, assumptions and beliefs are questioned, and habits of mind are ultimately transformed" (Taylor, 2009, p. 9). Through dialogue, students rewrote the internal scripts they held at the beginning of the student-teacher relationship to accommodate new understandings of themselves as learners. Learning conversations between students and teachers provided access to creative possibilities and enabled students to be known. Deborah discussed transformative learning in her practice:

> Part of transformative learning is perspective change; that's very big with our adults. There is the whole idea that they can really look at things differently, whether it's social repression or whether it's educational repression, which many of my students have had. Students look at their own concepts of themselves differently and start to say, 'Wait a minute. I am a smart person.' I've had adult students cry when they came to that realization. I also do psychoeducational assessments. When I would go over their testing with them and show them how intelligent they were, they would cry. No one had ever shown them that before. So, that starts the process of students examining assumptions about themselves, but beliefs about themselves don't just go away. It's not like, 'Oh, I'm all fixed now. Now I think of myself as intelligent and worthy.' No. The demons keep creeping in, and then we keep trying to work with the student to learn those demons are not true. It

goes back to positive regard. It's all interconnected in my mind. Larry Daloz talks about the mentoring role relationship. I would say that's the kind of thing I try to establish with my students, which is a combination of teaching and counseling.

When students were offered opportunities to explore deeply their abilities in a safe, judgement free environment, personal growth was the hallmark of success. According to Deborah:

> Personal growth is what I really love to see in a student. It seems like I should be saying, 'Oh, they can write better, and they can read well.' That's not my concept of success. The success is the inner transformation of the student, and that transformation has to be what they want to transform into. They become who they want to become, and they know that this is good. You know, most of them don't feel good enough when they come in, but they are good enough. They're more than good enough!

Leah pointed out that helping a student reframe their internal narrative was difficult. It competed with external academic expectations and the messages that the students' school histories had told them about their competencies and value as students:

> You can't destroy or undermine it completely. That's the academic system that they're part of, but you can put some perspective on it with students. 'This is the system

that we're talking about, and look how ridiculous this is!' I think the idea is about helping students realize the system and their inability to match the criteria that's been predetermined for them doesn't define them.

Leah described the impact of the complexities her students' mental health challenges when engaging in transformative education practices:

This population especially is filled with such shame about not finishing college yet - this sort of embarrassment of failure. Cutting through all that to have them work on the academics is often a challenge because part of them wants to do it and be successful, and then part of them is judging themselves.

Leah elaborated on the difficulties her students faced:

It's a lifetime of struggles! The negative thinking, the self-image, and the self-contempt all loop into their self-esteem issues, all tie to academic success. There's that disconnect between what the world thinks, 'Oh, you're so smart. Why can't you just blah blah blah?' and what the student experiences. 'Yeah, why can't I just?' It's still fitting the characterization of the external world. Any time they have a failure, they go back to the whole tape again. So, I make them aware of, 'You have this capability within you, and it has nothing to do with anything on the outside. It's all you.'

PERSPECTIVES ON ACADEMIC SUPPORT

Bridging academic expectations and the student's "ability to see themselves as capable and confident" was hard work. Leah expressed the students' needs to "get those decent grades" as validation and as a practical matter of passing courses.

Through the relationship, students were supported to take the small steps, the small risks that built competencies and new understandings of themselves. Chris reminded her students of the "whole picture" and then assisted them in identifying the details or "the details that were blocking them from seeing the whole picture. Those little successes along the way added up." Each of those successive steps made her students more aware of those details. According to Chris, the small, cumulative successes were the building blocks for rewriting her students' internal scripts. Chris continued to talk about the implications of transformative learning when dealing with the mental health issues of her students:

> Students trust me enough to tell me that they can kind of fall into a hole because I provide a safe place to come. It takes a while for that trust to build. I allow them to let out what's going on so they can get through it. It's hard to climb out and get back into the game after struggling with emotional issues. It's like a big monster is pulling your foot back down.

Sam also subscribed to the concept of building competencies through small steps. Each small step was a small success. In order to take small steps, her students:

… have to assert some point of action whether they're saying, 'I don't belong in this major, let me get out of here, or whatever. It's them taking the action and showing that they have the power to do something different. If they take action, things can work out.

Sam also pointed out that risking to take action, even to try small steps, was a leap of faith as well as, a choice:

It's a matter of showing there is hope that builds little successes. I think if you don't have hope, you can't make it. You look at each course they pass as actually a little step in the right direction. And you have to keep showing it to them, 'Oh look at how far along you've gotten. Look at what you've done.' Also, you have to say that you don't have to finish that. Giving them the option to choose to finish. They don't have to. It's because they want to. You have to cue into that.

The professors' extensive experiences reinforced their commitment to transformative education. Here are some of their final thoughts about transformative learning.

Frank stressed the importance of "building a relationship capable of potential forward growth" as fundamental to transformative learning. In the relationship:

Grades, promotions, licensure are all outward indicators of success, but the life-long 'success' could easily be the forging of relationship. A reticent adult buying into that relationship, increases the likelihood of growth.

Grace shared this regarding her students:

> I watch them become awake, and that is an amazing thing. And no matter what I teach, when I see that happen, it's like, 'Oh my god! Look what just happened!!'

Anne stated that she experienced the "greatest pleasure" when her students:

> Find acceptance of themselves; do what they want to do with their lives and not what other people expect them to do. Any time the student finds what they want to be and who they want to be gives me the greatest pleasure.

Sam asserted, "I am persistent, and believing in them—believing in their capability to change is an important strength I bring to my students." Deborah spoke for all the participants:

> I loved seeing the transformation. When they walked across that stage at graduation, that was just a symbol of it. Yes, my job was to help them succeed in college, and yes, they did, but even more important was the inner transformation that allowed them to walk across that stage. That was the greatest joy. That's the thing I loved most!

REFERENCES

Amabile, T. M. (2013). Componential theory of creativity. In E. H. Kessler (Ed.), *Encyclopedia of management theory*. doi:10.4135/9781452276090.n42

American Psychiatric Association. (2000). *Diagnostic and statistical manual of mental disorders (4th ed.).* Washington, DC: Author.

American Psychiatric Association. (2013). *Diagnostic and statistical manual of mental disorders (5th ed.).* Washington, DC: Author.

Americans with Disabilities Act (ADA) of 1990, PL 101-336, 42 U.S.C. §§ 12101 *et seq.*

Antshel, K. M. & Barkley, R. (2011). Children with ADHD grown up. In S. Goldstein, J. A. Naglieri, & M. DeVries (Eds.), *Learning and attention disorders in adolescence and adulthood: Assessment and treatment (2nd ed.) (pp. 113-134).* Hoboken, New Jersey: Wiley.

Barkley, R. A. (2010). *Taking charge of adult ADHD*. New York: Guilford Press.

Barkley, R. A. (2015). Emotional dysregulation is a core component of ADHD. In R. A. Barkley (Ed.), *Attention deficit hyperactivity disorder: A handbook for diagnosis and treat*ment (pp. 81-115). New York: Guilford Press.

Barkley, R. A. & Benton, C. M. (2022). Taking charge of adult ADHD: Proven strategies to succeed at work, at home, and in relationships *(2nd ed.).* New York: Guilford Press.

Bodensteiner, K. (2019). Do you wanna dance?:Understanding the five elements of dance. https://www.kennedy-center.org/education/resources-for-educators/classroom-resources/media-and-interactives/media/dance/do-you-wanna-dance/ Retrieved September 27, 2019.

Brendel-Scriabine, C.(2005). *Health in Connecticut*. Guilford, Conn:The Connecticut Humanities Council. http://www.cheritage.org. Retrieved January7, 2005.

Brown v. Board of Education, 347 U.S. 283, 74 S. Ct. 686, 98L.Ed. 873 (1954)

Brown, B. (2012). *Daring greatly*. New York: Avery.

Brown, T. E. (2013). *A new understanding of ADHD in children and adults: Executive function impairments.* New York: Routledge.

Brown, T. E. (2014). *Smart but stuck: Emotions in teens and adults with ADHD.* San Francisco: Jossey-Bass.

Brown, T. E. (2017). *Outside the box: Rethinking ADD/ADHD in children and adults.* Arlington, VA: American Psychiatric Association.

Community Mental Health Centers (CMHC) Act of 1963, PL88-164.

Cranton, P. (2006). *Understanding and promoting transformative learning: A guide for educators of adults (2nd ed.).* San Francisco: Jossey-Bass.

Dehart, D.& Iachini, A. L. (2019). Mental health and trauma among incarcerated persons: Development of a training curriculum for correctional officers. *American Journal of Criminal Justice* 44:457-473. https://doi.org/10.1007/s12103-019-9473-y Retrieved June 1, 2020.

Dix, D. (1843). *Memorial to the Legislature of Massachusetts.*

Fugate, C. M., Zentall, S. S., & Gentry, M. (2013). Creativity and working memory in gifted students with and without characteristics of attention deficit hyperactivity disorder: Lifting the mask. *Gifted Child Quarterly*, 57, 234-246. Doi:10.1177/00116986213500069

Gnezda, N. M. (2011). Cognition and emotions in the creative process. *Art Education*, 64(1), 47-52.

Goessling, D. P. (2000). From tolerance to acceptance to celebration: Including students with severe disabilities. In M. A. Winzer & K. Mazurek (Eds.), *Special education in the 21st century: Issues of inclusion and reform* (pp. 175-197). Washington, DC: Gallaudet University Press.

Grob, G. N. (1994). Mad, homeless, and unwanted: A history of the care of the chronic mentally ill in America. *History of Psychiatry, 17*(3), 541-558.

Grohs, M. (2017). The state of mental health in corrections. *Corrections Forum*. www.correctionsforum.net retrieved June1, 2020.

Hawes, J. M. (1991). *The children's rights movement: A history of advocacy and protection*. Boston: Twayne Publishers.

Hubbard, L. E. (2011). *ADHD and comorbid psychiatric disorders: Adult student perspectives on learning needs and academic support* (Doctoral dissertation). Available from ProQuest Dissertations and Theses database. (UMI No.3602610)

Individuals with Disabilities Education Act (IDEA) of 1990, PL 101-476, 20 U.S.C. §§ 1400 *et seq.*

Individuals with Disabilities Education Act Amendments of 1997, PL 105-17, 20 U.S.C. §§ 1400 *et seq.*

Individuals with Disabilities Improvement Act of 2004, PL108-446, 20 U.S.C. §§ 1400 *et seq.*

Joshi, G. & Wozniak, J. (2015). Bipolar disorder and ADHD: Comorbidity throughout the life cycle, In L. A. Adler, T. J. Spencer, & T. E. Wilens (Eds.), *Attention-deficit hyperactivity disorder in adults and children* (pp. 72-81). Cambridge, United Kingdom: Cambridge University Press.

Krone, B. & Newcorn, J. H. (2015). Comorbidity of ADHD and anxiety disorders: Diagnosis and treatment across the lifespan, In L. A. Adler, T. J. Spencer, & T. E. Wilens (Eds.), *Attention-deficit hyperactivity disorder in adults and children* (pp. 98-110). Cambridge, United Kingdom: Cambridge University Press.

Lamb, H. R. (2001). A century and a half of psychiatric rehabilitation in the United States. In H. R. Lamb & L. E. Weinberger (Eds.), *Deinstitutionalization: Promise and problems* (pp.99-110). San Francisco: Jossey-Bass.

Lawrence, R. L. (2008). Powerful feelings: Exploring the affective domain of informal and arts-based learning. *New Directions for Adult and Continuing Education*, 120 (Winter 2008), 65-77.

Lawrence, R. L. (2009). Intuition as a way of knowing. In C. Hoggan, S. Simpson & H. Stuckey (Eds.), *Creative expression in transformative learning: Tools and techniques for educators of adults* (pp. 129-143). Malabar, Florida: Krieger.

Lerner, B. H. (1996). Moonlight, magnolias, and madness: Insanity in South Carolina from the colonial period to the progressive era. *History of Medicine*, 125 (9).

Luchins, A. S. (1988). The rise and decline of the American asylum movement in the 19th century. *The Journal of Psychology, 122*(5),471-486.

Luchins, A. S. (1990). Moral treatment in asylums and general hospitals in the 19th-century America. *The Journal of Psychology, 123*(6),585-607.

Mechanic, D. & Rochefort, D. A. (1990). Deinstitutionalization: An appraisal of reform. *Annual Review of Sociology, 16*, 301-327.

Mezirow, J. & Taylor, E.W. (2009). *Transformative learning in practice: Insights from community, workplace, and higher education*. San Francisco: Jossey-Bass.

Mills v. *Board of Education of District of Columbia*, 348 F. Supp. 866 (D.D. C. 1972).

National Alliance for the Mentally Ill (NAMI). (2004). About mental illness. http://www.nami.org. Retrieved January 4, 2005.

National Mental Health Association (NMHA). (2005). NMHA and the history of the mental health movement. http://www.nmha.org. Retrieved January 4, 2005.

Paige, S. (1998). The devil in deinstitutionalization. *Insight*. http://www.psychlawg.org. Retrieved January 4, 2005.

Pear, R. (2004, July 8). Many youths reported held awaiting mental help. *New York Times*. http://www.namiscc.org. Retrieved March 22, 2005.

Pink, D. H. (2005). *A whole new mind*. New York: Riverhead Books.

Pliszka, S. R. (2015). Conceptual issues in understanding comorbidity in ADHD, In L. A. Adler, T. J. Spencer, & T. E. Wilens (Eds.), *Attention-deficit hyperactivity disorder in adults and children* (pp. 63-71). Cambridge, United Kingdom: Cambridge University Press.

Prince, J. B. (2015). Assessment and treatment of depressive disorders in adults with ADHD, In L. A. Adler, T. J. Spencer, & T. E. Wilens (Eds.), *Attention-deficit hyperactivity disorder in adults and children* (pp. 82-97). Cambridge, United Kingdom: Cambridge University Press.

Robinson, K. & Aronica, L. (2015). *Creative schools*. New York: Viking.

Robinson, K. & Aronica, L. (2013). *Finding your element*. New York: Viking.

Rothman, D.J. (1971). *The discovery of the asylum*. Boston:Little, Brown and Company.

Stainback, S., & Stainback, W. (Eds.). (1996). *Inclusion: A guide for educators*. Baltimore: Paul H. Brookes Co.

Treatment Advocacy Center. *Corrections Forum*. (2016). The treatment of persons with mental illness in prisons and jails: A state survey. www.correctionsforum.net. Retrieved June 1, 2020.

Tuckman, A. (2009). *More attention less deficit: Success strategies for adults with ADHD*. Plantation, Florida: Specialty Press.

Werner, E. (2004, July 8). Mentally ill youths 'warehoused'. *The Associated Press.* http://www.namiscc.org. Retrieved March 22, 20005.

Wechsler, D. (2008). *Wechsler Adult Intelligence Scale-- Fourth Edition (WAIS-IV)* [Database record]. APA PsycTests. https://doi.org/10.1037/t15169-000.

Wilens, T. E. & Morrison, N. R. (2015). Attention-deficit hyperactivity disorder and the substance use disorders in ADHD, In L. A. Adler, T. J. Spencer, & T. E. Wilens (Eds.), *Attention-deficit hyperactivity disorder in adults and children* (pp. 111-122). Cambridge, United Kingdom: Cambridge University Press.

Wright, W.D. & Wright, P. D. (2000). *Wrightslaw: Special education law.* Harbor House Law Press: Hartfield, Virginia.

Wright, W.D. (2005). Individuals with Disabilities Education Act of 2004. http://www.wrightslaw.com. Retrieved January 7, 2005.

ACKNOWLEDGEMENTS

Producing this book required a surprising amount of time. Originally, each chapter was meant to be an individual journal article. With each completed study, it became apparent to me that I could bind them together as a short, hopefully, accessible volume for both students and practitioners.

With deep appreciation, I must first thank the participants in each study. I am profoundly honored by their trust. In sharing their feelings about their experiences, courageously, the participants offer personal stories and incredible insights and perspectives with the intention to help others. Listening to their stories is truly transforming. Having such intimate access to the participants' experiences has forever changed my understanding of mental health challenges.

Next, I want to express my gratitude to my research assistant, Elizabeth Guerra, who insured the accuracy of my transcriptions. I also must thank my editor, Jane LaRoque, for her meticulous care in reviewing my manuscript. Lastly, with love, I am grateful to my family and friends for their unflagging support.

ABOUT THE AUTHOR

Laura Hubbard, Ph.D. is a long- standing faculty member at Curry College in Milton, Massachusetts. Dr. Hubbard is a full professor in the Program for the Advancement of Learning (PAL), an internationally recognized academic support program for college students with attention deficits (ADHD) and /or learning disabilities. Her particular focus at the college is adult learners with co-existing ADHD and psychiatric disorders and ways to support their progress towards finishing their degrees. Since earning a Ph.D. from Lesley University in Cambridge, Massachusetts, her research interests continue to involve expanding the understanding of complex adult learners.

www.ingramcontent.com/pod-product-compliance
Ingram Content Group UK Ltd.
Pitfield, Milton Keynes, MK11 3LW, UK
UKHW040738200225
455358UK00004B/147